Once Gay Always Gay?

HOMOSEXUAL TO HUSBAND

JEFF MORROW

Once Gay Always Gay?
Homosexual to Husband

Jeff Morrow
jeff@jeffmorrowministries.com
www.jeffmorrowministries.com
PO Box 985 Surry Hills
SYDNEY NSW 2010

Edited by Adrian Brookes
Design and layout by Ward Walker Design
Printed in Australia by NetPrint
Back Cover photo by Michelle Costelloe

ISBN 0-9757650-0-0

© Jeff Morrow 2005

Scripture quotations are taken from the
New King James Version and the
New International Version

All rights reserved. No part of this publication
may be reproduced, stored in a retrieval system
or transmitted in any form or by any means,
electronic, mechanical, photocopying,
recording or otherwise, without prior
permission of Jeff Morrow Ministries.Inc.

CONTENTS

FOREWORD BY JOHN KING — 1

PREFACE — 3
Why Me?

CHAPTER 1 — 7
Deception versus Truth: Believing The Lie

CHAPTER 2 — 27
Deception: Living the Lie

CHAPTER 3 — 43
Deception: The Truth Revealed

CHAPTER 4 — 61
Deception: The Price Paid

CHAPTER 5 — 71
Faith Versus HIV

CHAPTER 6 — 79
Fight or Failure

CHAPTER 7 — 93
Life with Lesley

CHAPTER 8 — 103
Things I've Learnt

CHAPTER 9 — 117
Walking Out a Miracle

ACKNOWLEDGEMENTS

When a book is written the author does not stand alone. It takes a team of committed people, in many cases loyal and loving friends, who encourage and support the author as he or she puts words to paper. I am no exception. This book was inspired by the encouragement of John King of International Men's Network, who insisted my story just had to be told. So I offer you my heartfelt thanks, John and Beccy King, for your friendship and support.

To all my friends at Hillsong Church and Christian Life Centre Mona Vale who have been with me on this wonderful journey called life, you know who you are. You are part of this book, and may God bless you.

DEDICATION

*To my darling wife, Lesley,
I dedicate this book to you.*

*You are an amazing woman of God
who exemplifies grace and beauty.*

*In the midst of overcoming
your own hurdles in life you
accepted me with all of mine
and have stood firmly
alongside me.*

*I could not have done this
without you.*

FOREWORD

I am very happy to write this foreword to, and recommend, the ministry of Jeff Morrow.

For years as head of the International Men's Network I have dealt with men from various backgrounds that are facing various issues. Issues that have ranged from addiction to murder, from petty thief to habitual lying.

All issues of character, all issues of sin.

One issue that has come up time and time again as 'too big' and 'too difficult' for most churches and ministries to handle was the issue of homosexual sin. First there was the 'we are born this way' argument. Then there was the 'God made me this way' excuse. Couple that with the barrage in the media and movies, and people have stopped thinking and just started accepting a very clear non-biblical practice as a normal everyday thing.

When my then PA, good friend and my daughters' nanny, Lesley came to me and said that she had met the man of her dreams, I was intrigued to meet him. When she told me that he was previously a practicing homosexual and was now one of Australia's longest surviving HIV positive people, I definitely wanted to meet him... and meet him NOW!!!

The man I met became a friend and fellow minister over the ensuing years. You ask Jeff his position and stand on homosexuality and he speaks with the authority and compassion that only experience and deliverance can bring.

He pulls no punches.

He makes no excuses.

Sin is sin and forgiveness, grace and hope are available to all who will repent and believe.

He is a man of character and conviction and this is a remarkable story of a journey that took him from Homosexual, to Husband.

John King
President
International Men's Network, Roanoke Texas
www.imnonline.org

PREFACE

Why Me?

Have you ever asked yourself why? Why did my life turn out this way? Why can't I have the things others take for granted?

There was a time when I asked myself these questions over and over again. They were the source of many years of heartache and tears because I couldn't find the answer. It would fill me with anguish to see a father hugging his children or to see a dad hold a small child in his arms. As a boy I had needed what that child was having, I had yearned for fatherly love and union but had always been denied it. Through all those years of longing I couldn't understand what I was missing and never knew what it meant to have a healthy, loving male-to-male relationship. For the 'fact' was – and I believed it to be an irreversible truth – I was gay.

Why did I have to be this way?

I pestered God for the answer. Eventually He began to reveal it to me – and it came as a big shock.

In this book I have been as honest and frank as possible. Some of it has been difficult to write and not everyone will agree with what I have written. I have tried to keep it simple so as to give as clear an understanding as possible about why I became gay. Knowledge brings understanding, understanding brings truth – and the truth will set *all of us* free to love the unlovely, the broken and the lost without judgement.

This is my story of how I had been totally deceived into believing I had been born gay and how God restored my life to what it should have been from the beginning. It tells how, through dysfunctional relationships, poor choices and the force of circumstances on a young and impressionable mind, I fell into homosexuality. As our society breaks down in these days of wilful rebellion against God, the homosexual lifestyle is becoming more and more common. Many young men and women do not have an inner peace about their sexuality and are not aware that there is a way to wholeness and peace.

These men and women do not need condemnation, mocking or segregation – they need to know there is a God who loves and accepts them just as they are.

"But God demonstrates His own love towards us, in that while we were yet sinners, Christ died for us. (Romans 5:8) If only they knew He is ready to walk with them through the deep issues that took them into that lifestyle, that He is a heavenly Father with a love and grace for them that cannot be fully experienced through any human relationship.

Due to its different extremes, homosexuality is a complex phenomenon, and yet it is also very simple. This sounds like a contradiction, but we must remember there are many different natures, personalities and circumstances at work and therefore many different reasons why a person becomes homosexual.

Yet when we get down to the deep issues we find a very similar story behind it all: a broken relationship with dad.

Hopefully as you read the ensuing pages any questions you may have had will be answered. You may be a Christian and find homosexuality abhorrent, you may be a leader and want to know how to minister to a gay friend, you may even be a pastor or leader who struggles with homosexual desires.

What you will find is how a gay man, who is HIV

Positive, had an encounter with God, had his life turned around, found a wife, overcame cancer, and started down the pathway of destiny that God had prepared for him.

There are many books on this subject by psychologists and highly gifted authors who have written in deeper detail. I have endeavoured to keep this book simple hoping to reveal the journey of recovery and discovery and spell out the lessons I have learnt on the way. Also I hope this book will encourage parents – especially fathers – to take a deep look into their relationships with their sons.

I am not proud of my past, but nor am I ashamed of my present – and I am excited about my future. "'For I know the plans I have for you," declares the LORD, "plans to prosper you and not to harm you, plans to give you hope and a future."' (Jeremiah 29:11.)

CHAPTER 1

Deception versus Truth: Believing The Lie

Paul de Jong, Senior Pastor of Christian Life Centre, Auckland, once hosted a group of street workers at a church function. He said of them,

'Each one of those people is possibly born with expectations of parents just like we were born. And yet somewhere along the way things happened, and it may have been in those early years that after they were born something violated who they were and they have ended up living a life that was far less than what it could be.

Our future is more often determined by the perceptions we believe to be true, than the truth itself.

We live in a world that has perceptions about life, and their perceptions (as we all have perceptions) to us are truth, but maybe are not reality, and are not real truths at the end of the day.

In fact, our perception, fact or fiction, has the power to rule our known world. And what God wants to do (particularly

with His leaders) is begin to shape our inner life so that He can change the external expression of who we are.'

Perceptions are rooted in beliefs – things we believe to be real, whether they are true or false; or in circumstances – situations we find ourselves caught up in. Perceptions are powerful: they determine our view of reality and shape how we see a topic, object or thing. 'As a man thinks in his heart…so is he.' (Proverbs 23.7)

When we perceive something – whether true or false – we allow ourselves to gain insight into the truth or to be deceived. False perceptions lead many into a deception that takes root in their being and ensnares them, diverting them onto a course in life that they were never intended to take.

Deception, according to the *Macquarie Dictionary*, means

- The act of deceiving someone
- The state of being deceived
- Something that deceives or is intended to deceive; an artifice; a sham; a cheat.

Since the beginning of time deception has ruled the hearts and minds of mankind, threading its way into choices that have led to brokenness and confusion. Ever since Adam and Eve were deceived by the serpent (Genesis 3:17), deception has caused individuals to believe what is not true or not to believe what is true. Deception leads its victim into incorrect and sin-filled choices or behaviour – and the terrifying part of it is that *through the power of deception, you don't know you are being deceived.*

While the power of deception misleads through lies and falsehoods, self-deception is the process by which we convince ourselves to accept as true or valid what is false or invalid. In other words, self-deception is the way we knowingly or not, justify our false beliefs. Self-serving people use false beliefs to meet or serve a need within them – and as we live in deception, through our choices and behaviour, we become deceivers by proxy, passing on our deceptions as truth to others.

Deception is the catalyst that sparked a broken humanity. It has drawn into captivity those who were looking for answers but had only themselves or others like them to rely on. Many have made decisions through deception, searching for truth, meaning and identity.

For the gay person searching for answers to their sexuality there is just one simple question: 'Was I born gay?' In this question lies the foundation of gay identity, and it was in the belief that I was born gay that all my rights as a gay man were based. I never understood it or even completely liked it, but I thought that if it was so I should simply accept it. It seemed I had always had same-sex attractions since I first became aware of them at the age of ten. They were all I could remember, and it therefore seemed self-evident that I had been born gay. It never occurred to me that my circumstances had fallen together in such a way as to form a huge deception; and as this deception was the first thing I held to be true, then the *real* truth had to counter it with an equally powerful response.

> **The only way to break deception is with Truth.**

Most of us can remember a few events from the latter part of our childhood – but what about those years we simply *can't* remember? It is rare that we remember much of those very early years of age five and under. We can't honestly recall our relationships with our parents or how influential, in particular, our father was throughout those years.

These, however, are the most important years of our lives for deciding what we will later become – the so-called 'formative years' of nurturing by mum and affirmation by dad. A child does not know its gender – its maleness or femaleness – at birth. Gender identity is imparted from parents, so if a parent is absent, or doesn't know how to impart it, how is a child to grow into a balanced person? Where is the role model?

This is why a gay man or woman will always tell you they were born that way. Because those early years of life are obscure, they can only remember same-sex desires and cannot trace the origins of them. Some children have male role models outside the family; some have no male influence at all but like to imagine what their dad would be like if they had one. Usually they imagine a strong, protective, loving man, a father who would play ball with them or join them in sports. Yet a child's imagination is a powerful thing and it can be a highly destructive influence. Our personalities are shaped by our social, cultural, emotional and intellectual surroundings. An environment of love and acceptance, where we have a caring and loving involvement with our parents, will be much more inclined to generate healthier perceptions, particularly about ourselves.

The Genesis of Deception

My Dad was a busy man. He was a mechanic, usually working on someone's car or helping my brother or doing something for Mum. Being the youngest I was often told to come back later, and I grew to feel I was a nuisance. The relationship between us was distant. He was not the type of man to display physical or even verbal love towards his children. It was very difficult to obtain the emotional warmth a child desires and in fact craves and needs. I was a shy child and would never force myself upon my father. My brother, however, was the opposite. He could get my father's attention at any given moment, and as my father was not a strong-minded person he would give in to him and do whatever he wanted. However, *attention does not necessarily mean affirmation or encouragement – it is just a focus.*

This reinforced my belief that my father loved my brother more than me, and my brother would aggravate this by throwing it in my face, sneering at me whenever he took Dad's attention away from me.

So if my father didn't love me, who could I find who would?

A child's thinking is not logical: it thinks by what it feels or sees. This is why it is crucial that parents speak words of love and affirmation and show their love through hugs and appropriate touch. The child will then learn what appropriate touch is and will recognise inappropriate touch if it is hugged or touched in that way.

We had just moved into a newly developing area. The old farms were being replaced by new homes. The dirt roads were being kerbed and sealed and the population was increasing as people moved into the area. Not far away from us there were neighbours whose boys I had befriended. One day I went to visit them, and the boys, who were in their young teens, encouraged me to take off my pants. In today's terms it would be seen as assault, but in those days these things were kept quiet and just seen as boys being boys. In a moment of time a child's innocence was lost forever. I started to learn things about sex that God never intended me to know. I was only ten years old, but even then I started to enjoy the fact that someone was interested in me as a person. I didn't think that what they were doing was wrong, I just saw it as some sort of affection, and any affection was better than none. As time went on I went back looking for this invalid affection.

When I was about sixteen one of the boys apologised to me and said he hoped it had not affected me. These boys had grown into young men and moved on, but for me the die was cast. I was stuck in immaturity as a boy and could not get out of it.

The tragic fact was, I wasn't looking for sex. I knew nothing about sex at that age – all I was looking for was the feeling of being wanted, and it was that physical touch, however inappropriate, that gave me the sense of belonging I craved.

The need to be loved is real for us all, even for a child, and I had learned a way of filling that need in my life. It wasn't right and it wasn't real, but it was at this point that I started to put up a barrier and subconsciously detach myself from my father. I had found that if my father could not love me or give me the attention I was seeking, there were others who could. Often a loveless void just needs to be filled, no matter how misconceived the love that fills it may be.

Defensive Attachment:

I am not the only member of my family who became gay – my brother did, too, but having different personalities we responded differently. I separated myself from my father and hated him, whereas my brother loved him dearly and would do anything to please him, even to the point of obsession. The same root cause – both of us wanted love and affirmation – led to different responses.

This inner withdrawal from my father is known as

'defensive detachment', in which I was subconsciously unwilling to relate any longer to my source of love because it had hurt me. For many young children this hurt is very real. It should never be seen as childish or silly, because it outworks itself long into adulthood in some form or other and healing cannot be achieved until the original hurt has been dealt with. Defensive detachment starts at such a young age that the child is unaware not only of what it is doing but also of the consequences of its choice.

The sad part about defensive detachment is that it destroys a child's ability to receive genuine love – which is what happened to me. The child's legacy is that it cannot relate normally with the same-sex parent and is inhibited in its ability to relate with people in general.

With defensive detachment, the natural need for love and identification with the same-sex parent goes unmet. The repressed desire for attachment to a father will outwork itself through an attachment to others of the same sex. And so the cycle continues as the child detaches itself from an unrewarding source of love and attaches itself to another. In this situation a young person, even one entering adulthood, is still looking for parenting. He or she is looking not only for love but also for identity and a sense of belonging in the family structure.

When this outworking manifests later in life it should be understood not as an adult phenomenon but as a child's defensive response coming out of hiding. Its power is rooted in previous hurts, which allow the past to control the present.

In my case my immature mind processed the lack of attention from my father into the conviction that he didn't love me. The sexual encounters I experienced at such a young age also stopped me from knowing how to place boundaries around my life. The desire for love or attention was more important than what was right or wrong. I didn't need love from my Dad; I had found it elsewhere, or so I thought, and it took many years for me to allow him back into my life, let alone my heart. I spent many years keeping him at bay.

The deception was starting to infiltrate my thinking. Why was I interested in men? Why did I desire to be held and hugged by the male person? I didn't understand, and it worried me to think that while my friends were flirting with girls I was secretly admiring my mates. I was starting to believe the lie that I had been born gay.

No matter how old we are, we all have a burning desire to be loved, valued and accepted. This desire is rooted in the soul, the inner core of our being. We are made for intimacy, and when this need is not met in appropriate ways – from loving parents, in the child's case – we seek to have it met in ways that will only lead us to destruction and brokenness. These destructive ways, reinforced by deception, develop into a pattern of learned behaviour. The strength of the desire for love leaves no room for rational thinking. I know I mistakenly referred to this new behaviour as my 'love language'.

If I had only known then that I was seeking my Dad's love, value and acceptance! But the damage had been done in the earliest years when Dad, due to the circumstances of his own life, gave his priority to working six days a week, leaving very little time for his children and family.

When I speak of needing a father's attention I am not talking of the demands that children put on their parents but of that father-and-son intimacy and trust that can only come from spending time together and from words spoken in one another's company. I really only knew my Dad as this person who would leave the house before I woke, arrive home too tired to communicate and was busy helping others on his days off. Yes, he did provide for his family and buy us material things, which I appreciated, but I still never knew my Dad as a son should know his father.

Just as Satan deceived Adam and Eve and broke their intimate relationship with God, the same deceptive spirit had severed the relationship between my father and me. I had believed the lie; I had unwittingly allowed Satan to become the ruler of my life, urging me to deny truth and head towards disobedience, despair and eventually, outside of God, death. I had been robbed and cheated of an intimate and wholesome relationship with my father, which in turn denied me the role model that should have helped me grow into a healthy heterosexual being.

Satan's plan has always been to separate, isolate and destroy. He did this in our relationship by creating a communication breakdown between my Dad and me. My Dad could not express his love physically or verbally. This kind of isolation creates a vacuum between father and son that God never intended but which we feel compelled to fill. When these vacuums remain unfilled the isolation and separation manipulates the messages the son perceives from the father, which can then start to saturate the child's senses and distort his emotions. The feeling of rejection can pervade the child's mind as it did mine. A feeling of loneliness – even though I was never physically alone – was a constant reminder of the lack of communication between my father and me.

Elizabeth R Moberley writes in *Homosexuality: A New Christian Ethic*,

'One may contrast children who are overtly deprived of the care of a parent with what might perhaps be termed "hidden orphans". These are the children of two-parent families who are no longer able to relate normally to one or other parent, and hence are unable to receive parental care even if the parent in question is present and offers care.'

A child that becomes isolated or separated from its parents in a shopping mall doesn't have the maturity to make wise choices. It will go with what feels right and gives comfort unless it has had training from its mum or dad to seek out a safe haven.

As we grow into adulthood we may find ourselves not only separated from our natural father but also from our heavenly Father. Finding unhealthy ways of meeting our genuine inner need starts to lead us down the path of self-destruction. As an example, young adults turn to drug or alcohol dependence, prostitution or robbery to satisfy the genuine craving within. As we step back we can see that homosexuality is another form of relational brokenness coming from a deep desire for love and acceptance – and for being valued by a loving dad.

> *A need will be filled, but the 'filling' is totally counterfeit.*

I had started high school and was struggling – academic pursuits were not my forte. My brother and sister were doing very well, especially my brother, as he would constantly remind me. Siblings can be cruel at times! I was starting to learn about sex and puberty, as one does around this time, although, as mentioned earlier, my initiation had already been forced upon me; and, having found out that a substitute could meet my need for fatherly love, I put into practice what I had learned. Sexual encounters with boys at school became a regular thing, but it came at a price. Mocking by other boys brought a confirmation that I must be gay or, as they termed it, 'a poofter' or 'queer'. This drove me further into myself. I knew of other boys who were labelled the same, so I spent most of my time with them. It just seemed to be the safest place to be.

This was the point where my desire for male love was eroticised. It was a learned practice that never left me until I met Jesus. It is like adding one and one together: you feel unloved or lonely; find a companion, have sex and this equals 'love'. A need will be filled, but the 'filling' is totally counterfeit.

School was not my scene, and even at a young age I was often seen as soft. Although I liked physical exercise I was not the football or cricket type as I didn't fit the mould of how young boys were supposed to be in those days. This brought on further mocking.

In fact, I loved sport, particularly athletics, so it was inevitable that I would join the local athletics club. Even though I had never thought I could excel at a sport of this nature, after school I would go off to training very eagerly. I was meeting new people and making new friends, which I enjoyed, but I also found I was making some new friends for the wrong reasons. Yes, I enjoyed the great mental release in running and I enjoyed the competition, but I was also attracted to the male form. I would often compare my looks to others, but somehow I never felt I was their equal. Even here I was having sexual encounters with other boys who eventually grew into mature men, married and had families. They saw these encounters as just adolescent sexual experiments and nothing more, whereas I was still trying to fill my inner need. I actually started to realise that I desired their physical touch, as I saw these boys not as boys but as men, more masculine than I was. Even at this point in my life I was still looking for the father figure.

This is often called the cannibal compulsion: we seek from others what we desire to have in ourselves or what we think we lack. From years of being told I was weak or soft and being called feminine names, particularly by my brother, I tried to draw my masculinity from others whom I saw as strong, masculine and handsome.

There was nothing within me that I could speak well of. I heard the boys I mixed with at the athletics meets receiving words of affirmation: 'Well done', 'You're a great kid', 'I'm proud of you', 'Love you, son'. It made me feel sad to hear them receiving words that built their self-esteem and confirmed their identities as sons and maturing young men. Many times I would ask my father to drive me to the athletic club and stay, but he would decline and give an excuse that my sister's boyfriend was coming over and he wanted to spend time with him or he had to meet with my brother – this was an excuse he continued for many years. Of course, my motive was that I just wanted to have my father with me, as many other fathers would be with their boys encouraging them as they competed. Even though I was still detaching from my Dad there was still working within me the natural desire for his company, to know he valued me, to feel I belonged and to gain his approval.

I would take myself to the athletics club feeling disappointed, convincing myself that my father was more interested in everybody else in the family than me. Once again, a child's thinking, but nonetheless real. I would walk home alone trying to be excited about my accomplishments but never showing it when I got home, as I felt nobody would be interested anyway.

As I internalised these thoughts they worked enormous damage to the view I took of myself. If we have spent many years internalising incorrect information, we must be realistic and understand it will take time to replace it with the truth. This comes about through acknowledging the problems, healthy relationships, counselling and the Word of God. Even though I was drawing away from my father I still had the inherent desire to receive his love and spend time with him. This I believe to be a God-given desire so that we are continually, throughout our lifetimes, trying to keep our love tanks filled. I know now that this love can only be fulfilled when we come to know Jesus.

At this point my mother, who had been ill for many years, had become bedridden and I still had no idea what was wrong. A friend of the family, a nurse for most of her working life, came to care for my mother. One day she came out of my mother's room, closing the door behind her, and phoned the doctor, saying, 'Mrs. Morrow had just passed away.' I remember going to the lounge room where my Dad was sitting. I sat beside him and he just cried. I can't remember that I cried over my mother's death until much later in life. Quite likely I did but just cannot remember it, as we often lock out the hurts of loss and grief when we are young only to have them surface later in life in some form or other. I was sent to stay at a relative's home with my sister till the funeral was over. I was not allowed to attend the funeral, and consequently felt I never had the opportunity of saying goodbye to my mother. It left a great void in my life. I was thirteen years old.

The last few paragraphs have signalled some crucial issues. For a child, exclusion fosters a sense of isolation, of not belonging, which I felt not only at the time of my mother's funeral but also at other times when I was barred from family issues. This continued well into my adult life. My family never sat around the dinner table and spoke of life, finances, how we felt, or emotions. The result was that I entered adult life without basic life principles and, more importantly, without the ability to communicate with others. My father never showed emotion, so neither did I. I saw how my father behaved and subconsciously role-modelled myself on him by also being emotionless and withdrawn. My brother's constant mocking made me feel a lesser person, destroying any self-esteem I may have been developing. The ridicule from the boys at school at being gay just confirmed that I was different and drove me to the ones who accepted me. Instead of being able to stay around healthily developing males I was pushed into hanging out with broken people just like me.

Repetitious words can be life changing, and exclusion from family is soul destroying. They can force a child or young teenager into irrational decisions. 'Death and life are in the power of the tongue:…….' (Proverbs 18:21)

My mother died of uraemia, or kidney failure. After her death my father's sisters came to help out, but it was difficult for them due to their age. After a short time I was sent away to live with relatives. The very time I needed my father most was the time I was separated from him. For many years I could not understand how a father could do this. He told me years later when I confronted him about it that he had been talked into it by the family and relatives, admitting that in hindsight he had made the wrong choice.

I eventually left school a scarred and insecure person, having no real friends, just acquaintances, walking into life feeling totally alone and vulnerable to whatever lay ahead.

Circumstances, experiences and words spoken to me had permeated my very being and convinced me I had been born gay. The lie had firmly taken root; the seeds of deception had grown ever so quickly so that by the time I entered the adult world all the negative and deceptive influences were set in place in my life. Looking back I can see I was set up with all the elements of failure: separation from family, broken relationships, no self-esteem, a worthless self-image. Sadly I had learned to use my body as the only means of meeting my need to be loved.

I was secretly living a double life, having no vision for marriage or children of my own or grandchildren. I lived with the shame of lying to cover the secret of my lifestyle choices. I lived a life of meaninglessness that had cheated me out of my inheritance as a man.

CHAPTER 2

Deception: Living the Lie

Don Walker writes in *Arrows of Truth,*

We like to think that we can separate private from public concerns, character from performance, worldview from responsibility. Regardless, what we do is not simply affected by what we think, it is determined by it. What we think – even when we are not fully aware of what it is that we've been thinking – shapes our perceptions, our preferences, our prejudices, and our priorities. What we think will determine not only how we interpret what we see, hear, and feel, but how we react to those sensations. Even if we never actually think about what we think, it is at work in us in a dramatic way. In a very real sense, we are what we think.

It could be said that embracing a lie allows us to live in a way that suits us, or that putting on a façade can bring an appearance of security, strength and purpose to our lives. However, the emptiness that filters through the heart and soul will not be satisfied. The soul is not fooled by façade and still longs to fulfil its desire for a real purpose, for something – some relationship – it was created to be in union with. I wanted to be in union with my Dad.

When people embrace a lie they tend to hold out against the truth no matter how blatantly obvious the truth may seem. To renounce the lie and embrace the truth could challenge them to make some very difficult and uncomfortable behavioural changes. It is much easier to stay in the old fleshly syndrome of 'leave me as I am in my comfort zone with all my familiar lifestyle and surroundings'.

Truth can stare us in the face, but acknowledging it can be too painful. Too often we opt for the easy way out which, at the time, seems pain-free but in reality keeps us in bondage.

It appears to be a fact of life that people find it much easier to believe a lie they've heard many times over than a truth they've never heard before. Even after reading this book there will still be those who refuse to believe that change from homosexuality to a normal heterosexual lifestyle is possible. It would take a complete paradigm shift for them to even consider the possibilities.

My early sexual encounters, my desire to be emotionally connected to a male, others' accusations that I was gay – these had all prepared me to believe I had indeed been born gay. Now I was ready to take hold of the lie, to make decisions by it and live as though it was true.

We must remember that a lie is not always told in words. Some of the worst lies of all are communicated or acted out in secrecy or silence, which just as effectively creates seeds of deception. We can convince someone they are worthless simply by giving nothing of ourselves to them: no time, attention, affection, warmth, correction or affirmation – in short, no love – to neglect them to the point where isolation and separation consume them.

For me personally, believing this lie made me susceptible to its power. I was now firmly convinced I was gay. The lie became truth to me, and I took on the gay identity as an assumption of fact.

Our identity is the way we see, hear and feel about ourselves. Self-image is just one aspect of identity, which also involves the groups we feel part of and the significant aspects of ourselves that we use when we describe ourselves to others. I described myself as gay because that is how I saw and felt about myself: 'We are what we think', whether or not what we think is true.

We all have collective, social and personal identities that link up to describe who we are and how we fit into a society or social group. In common with everyone else, my identity was compounded and reassured by the company I was keeping and the places I visited, which reinforced the way I felt about myself. The 'thinking' is at work in us, subconsciously or not.

Identity Theft

In this world we have what is known as identity theft. This style of crime is growing at alarming rates and no one is guaranteed of protection from it. But how can someone steal your identity? Identity theft occurs, for example, when someone uses your personal information without your knowledge or consent to commit a fraud or theft. They do this by stealing key pieces of personal information, either physically or in some other way. They then use it to impersonate you and commit crimes in your name – and the interesting thing is that these thieves may never see your face but they know everything about you.

Scary, eh? Your good name has gone bad, your credit rating is down the drain and you are left to pick up the pieces and get your life back on track. In reality your whole being has been violated and you no longer feel safe or protected. Vulnerability and fear creep into your life. You have lost your identity, something you always believed was sacred.

'The thief comes only to steal and kill and destroy...' (John 10:10) Satan does this by robbing us of our identity, and if he succeeds, we, because of our desire for love, value and acceptance, become vulnerable to accepting another identity which we believe can bring us what we desire. It is also interesting to note that, according to John 10:10, Satan isn't satisfied with just stealing, he then tries to complete his work by killing and destroying. Some victims of identity theft have found the repercussions horrendous and the financial devastation soul-destroying. The thief was not satisfied with the mere theft, just as Satan was not satisfied with stealing my identity. His work continued to worm its way through my life, bringing me to the point of suicide.

Identity Confusion

This is the time, usually in adolescence, when a person consciously takes on the role of discovering who he or she is and who they could be in the world. For a young person struggling with same-sex attraction it can be a time of confusion and self-recrimination about why they feel different. Often they try to establish who they are by associating with people of the same orientation and values, forming cliques where they find security and comfort. The clique, significantly, offers a haven of acceptance and belonging.

A major part of the adolescent's quest for identity and sense of place in the world is the search for sexual and social meaning. Those with a same-sex attraction often experience a sense of alienation together with a dislike not only of what they are feeling but also of what they are doing. The desire for sexual indulgence and gratification, together with the feeling of it being wrong and not normal, clouds the mind and creates further confusion.

Identity in Christ

The 'Who am I?' question is one that applies not only to adolescents but also to adults who have never found a place of belonging and acceptance. They won't discover their true identity until they find out who they are in Christ, for only then do we find out who we were created to be and the meaning and purpose of our lives. If you ask them who they are, most people will probably tell you what they do for a living – a singer or an actor, for example – but that is not who they are, it is what they do. The gift or ability that enables us to earn a living may well be God-given, but it still does not define our identity. Satan's intent is to steer us away from finding our true identity that was completed on the Cross of Calvary.

Understanding our identity in Christ is crucial to our success at living the victorious Christian life, no matter what lifestyle we have come from. The security, significance and assurance that a child needs from a father can only come from a father who fully knows the inner needs of a child.

I have seen my identity unfold as I have continued to build my relationship with God. The first revelation was to find that I have a Dad who loves me and shines His love upon me – a Father who calls me a son and a child of God. He's my Dad who I can come to for guidance in times of need, but also when I just want to talk to Him as a son talks to his earthly dad. (John 1:12) I now need have no fear of approaching God:

- I am holy and acceptable to God (justified) (Romans 5:1)
- I have been adopted as Christ's child (Ephesians 1:5)
- I have been bought back (redeemed) and forgiven

of all my sins (Colossians 1:14)
- I am complete in Christ (Colossians 2:10)

Though I remember that my previous lifestyle was an abomination to Him and frowned upon by many, I am now set free of it, for nowhere in the Bible does God condemn the person – He only condemns the sinful sexual act. As the apostle Paul writes in 1 Corinthians 6:10 after naming all those who would not see the kingdom of God, 'And that is what some of you were. But you were washed, you were sanctified, you were justified in the name of the Lord Jesus Christ and by the Spirit of our God.'

Moving On

After leaving school I entered the motor industry, as cars had been a family interest for many years, and as my Dad was a mechanic I thought it might give us a common interest. It was at this time that my sporting focus changed from athletics to motor racing, which I pursued with a passion.

I bought a racing car and, with the help of some friends I had made through work, established a team. Working on the car was one of my greatest delights, and as soon as one race meeting was over I would start preparing for the next.

My Dad never had much belief in me as a mechanic. Many times he would either ask me to leave it to my crew, or if I continued he would take over the job himself. This did not help our relationship at all. However, my driving ability was something he could not refute, as I came home with trophies and great results.

It was interesting to note that Dad would gather the information from my crew, never from me. Though he would tell others of my accomplishments, and tell them with pride, not once did my father congratulate me or show any approval of me. Years later I found out from my brother that Dad would take my trophies to work to show his mates. However, it was not his mates who needed to hear about his pride in my accomplishments – it was me.

I was eighteen years old and living a double life. Through the day I was this straight guy working in a predominantly male industry, yet after hours I was a gay man hanging out with other gay men. The only affirmation I received was after I had handed my body over. My circle of gay friends was expanding and it wasn't long before I was enticed into a world of bars, clubs and bathhouses. I was now in an environment that accepted me for who I was, where there was no judgement or condemnation or being laughed at or mocked for being different. This world of acceptance and free love was nothing but a fantasy, as reality was still there and would often hit back and hit hard. It was a life that was purely sexual, based on how attractive your body was. Every night was a meat market – men standing in bars, clubs and bathhouses with an invisible sign saying, 'Choose me, I want to be loved, even just for a moment,' flaunting their sexuality but unwittingly revealing their brokenness and their silent, lonely lives.

To those who find this hard to understand, remember this: every night young men and women go to singles bars and do exactly the same thing, but under the guise of heterosexuality. Somehow this makes it acceptable. To think that because you are heterosexual you cannot be broken inside is a lie. The fruit of brokenness may be different, but the seed – love deprivation, demeaning words, abuse (whether physical, verbal or emotional) – that was planted in childhood is the same. Some choose sex, drugs, rebellion, promiscuity, control or manipulation and others go through life never being able to keep a marriage or relationship together.

For ten years I wandered in and out of full-on gay relationships. They were years of jealousy and emotional upheaval, definitely years I would rather forget for many reasons, but years that were crucial in bringing me to the point of questioning the meaning of life and even life itself. The continual secrecy of hiding my lifestyle hung like a cloud over my head. The fear of anyone finding out, particularly my straight friends or workmates, was a heavy burden.

When two broken same-sex people try to build a relationship, there is no foundation for it to work from, as the relationship was never intended from the time of creation. The sad part is that they never see their brokenness. Hurt people tend to hurt people; this is the norm for their life, and to expect anything better is like a cat chasing its tail. There is no benchmark to provide a standard, because it was man and woman who were meant to form a union, not man and man or woman and woman. If you were to ask any gay person they might silently agree, but to draw an honest answer from them would mean they would have to doubt their sexuality and confront the possibility they could be wrong. We all know pride comes from its author, Satan, and for my part I could not see God's design until He revealed it to me. Most gay people would come back with the same old rationale: 'I was born gay, so it must be from God, so it must be okay.'

Both partners in a homosexual relationship have similar needs, but the deficits in their lives make each unable to meet the other's needs. The detachment or hurt that originally stopped the natural growth into heterosexuality may come to the surface and break the relationship, creating the roller-coaster ride that often comes with same-sex relationships and no doubt quite a few heterosexual ones as well.

After many years of failed attempts to gain approval from my Dad, I closed my heart totally to him, and also, to a degree, to my brother. The hate turned to a root of bitterness, savage and real. I have heard a root of bitterness described as 'anger with a history'.

I was thirty-four years old, my motor racing career had come to a close after sixteen years, I groaned at the thought of having to see or even speak to my father and I was alone. The only reason the relationship with my brother was kept alive was that we shared the same lifestyle.

> **We often choose people out of our brokenness.**

Male flatmates came and went from my home. Often we choose people out of our brokenness instead of out of common sense and wisdom, and because of my poor choices they usually left me in a worse financial situation than when they arrived.

I struggled through the next six years, eventually having to sell my home. In an effort to start a new life I left the country and moved to Fiji. While I was there God drew me to church through the inspiration of the island music, bringing me to tears every time I heard the word 'love' sung or spoken. Then, one-and-a-half years later, still broken and penniless, He brought me back to Australia to start the healing process. The running was over, the forms of escapism ceased. Everything I had worked for in my life was gone.

> *How could anyone love me? I was a homosexual.*

When I returned to Australia I had nowhere to live except at my father's house with a man I hated. Life was at an all time low.

Driving home one day after a failed and miserable suicide attempt, I stopped at a church and asked to speak to someone. To me I was entering what I had thought of as enemy territory, as all my life I had been told that God hated homosexuals. I had grown up in the early sixties, when being gay was not as accepted, even in worldly society, as it is now. It was hidden from other family members and definitely not the sort of thing to be spoken about. Even though my family may have had their suspicions about me, the subject was never raised.

At the church a man beckoned me in to his office, greeted me and hastened to tell me that God had told him someone was coming and that he should wait. Yeah, sure! was my thought. However, when I started to break down and tell him my whole story, all he could say was that Jesus loved me, and so did he. How could anyone love me? I thought – hadn't he heard me say I was a homosexual? In the world's eyes that meant the scum of the earth, to be mocked and ridiculed, smiled at in person and scorned in private.

Breaking the old, receiving the new

But there I stayed for two hours, crying from the depths of my being. I went home and cried for another thirteen hours. I slept and cried, with my father asking occasionally if I was all right. This was an experience I will never forget, for in those hours God started something that changed the course of my life. Just a short time later I was sitting in church and the pastor made an invitation for those who wanted to give their lives to the Lord to come forward. At first I couldn't move; it was as though I was stuck to the seat. Then I looked at my hand, and on my finger was a ring that a past male friend had given to me. I took it off, put it in my pocket and instantly I was free to walk to the pulpit and receive Jesus as my Lord and Saviour. This ring had been a silent covenant of a former relationship, and its influence had to be broken. Now I was entering into a new covenant with Jesus, a covenant of reconciliation and unconditional acceptance, even though I was still a very broken person. Over the next few months I was desperate to be healed of my broken sexuality. All I wanted was to be normal, to be set free to live the life I had dreamt about.

Salvation is the beginning of the healing process, not the healing itself. Healing takes time and can be a roller coaster ride. God uses a process unique to each individual, and for me it was an inner healing programme that dealt with all the issues separating me from the intimacy I needed from my father and the resulting resentment and hatred I had for him. The biggest issue I had to face was forgiveness.

With Open Eyes

I never knew how broken I was till I examined myself from a different perspective with a new set of eyes. It is only when you accept Jesus as Lord that the Holy Spirit gives you new eyes to view yourself with. He brings illumination to sin and reveals the need of a Saviour.

I engaged myself in a programme that dealt with relational brokenness. I didn't know what to expect, but I didn't really care – I just wanted to be free. I learned later that being sexually broken is really a relational problem and that the fruit from it can evolve in a sexual nature. I was hoping God would just move His finger and I would be free, but what I was to experience became a real eye opener.

CHAPTER 3

Deception: The Truth Revealed

'Telling the truth has enormous power to it. By revealing a truth, you are giving it substance. Giving it substance and power may also take the fear out of something that has been running your life for a long time. That's the liberation of it.'
– Arthur H, *'Newslink'*, 2000.

A profound truth can have two sides to it, a negative and a positive. How you view such a truth can determine which side of it you take hold of. The negative side may offer a way of avoiding pain or hardship, while the positive side may lead through suffering to a vision of joy at the end.

A truth, then, can be liberating or devastating. It can bring incredible joy or sadness. I remember being told I had cancer; I wanted it to be a lie, but it was a truth that brought me great sorrow and bondage. I lived in bondage to chemotherapy for several months. This period of my life revolved around hospital appointments, the effects of the chemotherapy and trying to hold down my job.

Yet despite this, the truth – after the initial shock – ushered in a strategy for a total healing that remains to this day. Could this have happened if I had denied the problem, believing it would just go away?

A lie revealed does bring pain, but with it comes a belief that you are now empowered to challenge not only the lie but also the author of it. Imagine you found out your child was addicted to drugs. First there would be the pain of finding out, then the process of challenging the child and the implementation of therapy. The process would open the way for the underlying issues to be exposed and addressed, resulting in the restoration of a life and family relationships.

Restoration Outworked

One night after I'd been reading of a man who overcame homosexuality, God gave me a revelation about what had brought about my brokenness. While I was sleeping I saw a number of pictures of past experiences going right back to when I was very small. I saw myself as a child being ridiculed and shouted at by my family. They were calling me a nuisance and other things that were cruel for a child to hear and telling me to go away, resulting in the isolation and separation I have already mentioned. I had never experienced a vision like that before and it seemed to last for hours, going from one scene to another. It was like watching a PowerPoint presentation of my life.

I was so angry because this vision showed me that my brokenness could have been avoided if my Dad had been a father to me, if he had protected me from my brother's cruel words and not laughed in agreement, if he had hugged me when I was little and spent time with me as a dad should.

However, God placed in my spirit that although the causes were outside my control I had to take responsibility for my choices and responses. I didn't feel I should because I felt my father was to blame, but God was clearly saying that the decision to carry out my choices was totally my doing. If this were so, then it would be my choice to turn my life around. I had found the truth that I had lived a lie, *and now this newly discovered truth would be the catalyst that would bring to fruition the desire and discipline for change.*

Deuteronomy 30:19 says, 'This day I call heaven and earth as witnesses against you that I have set before you life and death, blessings and curses. Now choose life, so that you and your children may live.'

The Power of Taking Responsibility

We are answerable for things that are within our power

to control or manage. Therefore we have the power of choice: we can make a conscious decision to change the way we are and to change our future. This is why God impressed on me the importance of taking responsibility for my own choices. When I did it empowered me to rise above obstacles, to face with confidence the process of change even though I did not know what lay ahead or what I would have to deal with. Taking responsibility says you become a partaker in your own destiny alongside God.

Was it anyone else's fault that I lost my life's savings? Was it anyone else's fault that I chose the wrong flatmates? Was it anyone else's fault that I... *No!* It was my own responsibility, and knowing this set me free to rejoice in the future. Taking charge of my choices makes me a stronger person because it gives me the hope that I can fulfil my dreams.

Taking responsibility for our own choices is a road to joy and happiness and a source of self-esteem. It enables us to shape our destiny and, most importantly, to build our character because we know what we are willing to stand and fight for. It is vital to understand that taking responsibility is a key to our successes, whether in relationships, personal development or our life's goals in general.

Taking responsibility is saying 'no' to blaming others.

Shifting blame can be very destructive, as it not only destroys self-esteem but it also creates anger and resentment and can wreck relationships. When I take responsibility for something, I know I am affecting not only the people around me but also the environment I live in. It strengthens me to face life's challenges.

So here I was, living in a house with a man I hated, and here was God saying I could not continue to hate him even if I felt justified. As I moved through the programme on relational brokenness we came to a part entitled 'Forgiving Others'. God was pressing me very firmly to approach my father about my life and our relationship. I fought against it for weeks, but as my trust in God was growing, and because I was desperate for healing, I came to the point where I asked my Dad to sit with me before he went to my sister's house for tea.

> *It is amazing how a moment in time can repair years of pain, just by humbling oneself and asking forgiveness.*

What happened next no-one would have expected. As I sat down beside him (a miracle in itself), the words that flowed out astounded even me. I had asked God to give me the words to speak because mine would have come out in anger – and He did. 'Dad, I've hated you for most of my life. Please forgive me for the way I responded to you.' Here I was asking my Dad to forgive me, a total reversal of what I'd thought should have been said, but God knows best. This was followed by a very long talk about our life and relationship. I was able to express all my pain; I felt it was fine to speak it out, and I did so with no condemnation, just as a father and son should be able to talk. In the end I asked a simple question: 'Dad, why did you treat me this way?' His answer pierced my heart: 'Because that's how my father treated me.'

I didn't expect it. I was crushed, and my heart sank. Anger and bitterness turned to compassion and then love. You see, my Dad lived in bondage, too. His brokenness was different from mine but carried the same longing for love. How he must have felt, not to be able to express his feelings all his life and to feel the love from his own father. This moment in time was the beginning of us growing together as father and son and the beginning of my healing. I discovered how amazing it is that a moment of time can repair years of pain just by humbling yourself and asking forgiveness.

'For if you forgive men when they sin against you, your heavenly Father will also forgive you. But if you do not forgive men their sins, your Father will not forgive your sins.' (Matthew 6:14-15)

The Power of Forgiving

We often think that forgiving someone who has hurt us is giving in to the enemy and being weak – that we are letting the culprit go free. The reality is that we are setting ourselves free from the past and refocusing on the future. All of us at some time in life have experienced hurt and trauma, but how long are we to live in this pain that will eventually eat us away? How often have we seen hurt people living their lives out of the pain of past experiences such as abuse or marriage failure? Holding on to the pain perpetuates a curse over ourselves. It creates within us the thought patterns and emotions that cause us to act out of our pain and respond to situations out of the brokenness within us. So how long do we hold on to this pain and refuse to forgive? The answer depends on how long we want to live in bondage and be controlled by the problems of others. We may feel, as many do, that we have a right and responsibility to hold on to this anger. The truth is that it is out of our sphere of responsibility. Their judgement will come from God.

We can put so much physical and emotional energy into vengeance that it leaves us nothing to reconstruct our life. Medieval literature speaks about the 'worm that eateth

> *'To err is human, to forgive, divine.'*
> – Alexander Pope

from within', and I think this paints a very good picture of unforgiveness and the energy it takes to hold on to it. Its power works insidiously, turning full circle until victims become persecutors themselves. In short, they become just like the ones they resent.

When we choose not to forgive we live in anger, bitterness and self-pity. We hide behind a wall of continual defensiveness, justifying ourselves repeatedly. All this does is to reveal our true selves, whereas forgiving reveals Christ. Unforgiveness says I will live in sin with a divided heart, but forgiving says I will live with a united heart in the wholeness of Christ, willing not to judge others for their failings, as I don't want to be judged for mine.

'But I say to you, love your enemies, bless them that curse you, do good to them that hate you, and pray for them which despitefully use you, and persecute you; that you may be the sons of your Father which is in Heaven' (Matthew 5:44-45)

The power of forgiveness started to bring healing and freedom. I was now able to face the issues that were crucial for me to be freed from homosexuality, even though I still didn't feel that Dad deserved my forgiveness. The fact was that Jesus didn't need to forgive me, either, but He did, unconditionally, and so must I. I also forgave my brother and we became great buddies. My Dad? Well, outside of Jesus and my wife he is my best friend and I love him so much. I have finally found my Dad who loves me and has always loved me, a dad who would have done anything for me if he had only known how. Sadly, my perception of him was one of the things that had added to the damage.

Remember: perceptions are rooted in beliefs – things we believe to be real, whether they are true or false; or in circumstances – situations we find ourselves caught up in.

Having understood the power of forgiving others, I was now able to forgive myself. I had made some bad choices, but once I had come to know why I made them I was able to set myself free, no longer walking in condemnation but in the freedom of Christ.

My Dad's treatment of me proved the law of reproduction. His father reproduced a copy of himself in my Dad and my Dad reproduced a copy of himself in me.

The first law of God is that like produces like, except that we often don't think of it in terms of emotions or behaviour. If this law works in the spiritual, it must also work in the natural, so if you see yourself in your children and don't like what you see, don't try and change them – change yourself, as they will only copy what they see in you!

I remember sitting in a counselling session when the counsellor asked me if I was a 'wanted' child. I choked on the words, for I had never felt wanted. I had never been able to raise the question with my Dad, and now it seemed irrelevant. I have had to deal with my self-esteem by understanding that who I am in this world is of no consequence, it is who I am in Christ that is important. It is not important what *people* say about me, it is important what *God* says about me. I am learning what it is to be a man from God's perspective; learning who my heavenly Father is, surrendering to His will and, most importantly, *allowing* Him to be my Father.

> *'You can't talk your way out of problems you've behaved yourself into.'* – Stephen R. Covey

Surrendering our will to God doesn't say we are weak in any way whatsoever. What we are saying is that our future is more important than our past or present and that we acknowledge a problem in our lives. This is the first step to healing, for it engages the power of change.

For me, change came by making hard calls, by putting learned habits to death and replacing them with wise choices in life; and the walk continues.

Understanding that I am a new creation was imperative to making new choices, ones that went against everything I had lived for previously. I was now looking through new eyes which put a new perspective on everything and showed me that every action I had engaged in triggered an equal and corresponding reaction. Our perspective on things comes from the beliefs we have acquired, whether true or false. This is why Romans 12:2 is so important to grasp: 'Do not conform any longer to the pattern of this world, but be transformed by the renewing of your mind. Then you will be able to test and approve what God's will is – his good, pleasing and perfect will.

> *'It's all about habit replacement creating new routines and making new choices'*
> – Di Wilson

Power of Choice

'This day I call heaven and earth as witnesses against you that I have set before you life and death, blessings and curses. Now choose life, so that you and your children may live.' (Exodus 30:19)

In the Scriptures God shows us clearly that our choices will have an everlasting effect on our destiny. He also shows us that when He spoke of life He was covering not only our health but also relationships, destiny, finances and all other aspects of life. Our choices define who we are, what we believe in and who or what we become. Every day we are faced with issues that have to be dealt with by choice. Not responding to these issues is making a choice *not* to choose. This can lead us into a sense of hopelessness as we abdicate the responsibility for our choices to others in our life. In short, we lose control over our destiny and allow others to shape it.

Even though our circumstances seem out of our control, we still have to choose how to respond to them, and it is our perceptions that determine how we respond. Perceptions are our keys to choosing whether we will be a victor or a victim, whether we will see the glass as half full or half empty. If we can think positively about a negative circumstance, we create the opportunity to grow in character. Probably few would choose to stagnate, and would rather take the attitude of 'I am going to take this bad situation and turn it around so I learn and benefit from it'. This type of thinking benefits not only the person directly involved but also those around them. Through the one's example others can experience the meaning to life by entering into their destiny as well.

The circumstances of your childhood may have affected your thinking, lowered your self-esteem and pointed you in a direction that has not been good. However, the key to how it all turns out is not what has happened to you but how you respond to it – and you hold that key in the power of your choice. The facts may be that you have been abused emotionally, physically or sexually. The truth is you don't have to stay hurt or angry because you have the choice not to be.

To say 'I have to' can become a bondage, but to say 'I choose to' gives us the liberty to explore life-changing directions. Right from the beginning of creation God gave man the freedom to choose, and He won't take it back; it is sacred to Him. Often our choices are taken from the view we have of ourselves. The Bible says, 'As a man thinks in his heart, so is he.'

You can become anything you want to be by the way you think of yourself. If you think small, then small you will be. However, if you think big and beyond the box, if you believe God is greater than any obstacle, that there is a bigger picture to your life than the things you can see, then you will be big and all things will become possible. This is where choice can be determined and you can design your destiny. The power of choice coupled with responsibility is one of the greatest assets God has given us – so use it and use it wisely, remembering you reap what you sow.

Reconciliation to Recovery

One night while I was reading, God spoke into my spirit, saying, 'When you won your first 100 metres race as a child, I was there. When you wheeled your racing cars onto the track for the first time, I was there and I was proud of you. When you cried in desperation for love, I was there.' I wept so hard and then I knew through revelation that my heavenly Father was my Dad. He has emotion, He laughs and He cries with me, He watches over me, He desires so much for me and He guards me. I asked God to give me friends of His choosing who would be best for me, as I knew if I made the choice I would only choose them out of my brokenness. The people He chose were crucial in helping me become whole as they treated me as an equal, a man, and encouraged me. It was through their acceptance of me as I was, with all my baggage, that I started to view my self in a new light.

Elizabeth R Moberley writes in *Homosexuality: A New Christian Ethic*, 'It is the provision of good same-sex relationships that helps to meet unmet same-sex needs, heal defects in the relational capacity, and in this way forward the healing process.'

With God putting His love, His Word and His chosen

people around me, I started growing and maturing into the person He wanted me to be, not forgetting that I had to do my part as well. Remember: take responsibility, choose wisely and lay down old habits. My life's walk is still going along with me making godly choices. The road has had its obstacles, but what road doesn't have them?

Reconciliation's Outstretched Arm

During the course of my healing I was going back to Fiji for a visit. As the bus approached to take me to the airport I turned around to say good-bye. Then Dad walked up to me and put his hand out to shake mine. I almost cried.

I was forty-five years old and it was the first time I can remember that we physically touched. (A handshake is the norm for us now when we part.) Life was looking good. I had peace, hope and a dad.

Relationships of any sort can only be repaired if someone puts out their hand – either a hand *of* hope or a hand *for* help, it doesn't matter which. Jesus put out His hand of hope to me and I put out my hand for His help.

I have had a number of gay men come to me asking, 'Why doesn't God just change me?' A fair enough question, for if God wants wholeness for all mankind surely He could just restore our broken sexuality in a moment of time?

The reasons I see are firstly that we would just carry our rejection, bitterness, low self-esteem, behavioural attitudes and so on with us. What would be the point if God had just turned me instantly into a heterosexual man? I still would have carried hatred for my Dad, still been resentful towards my brother, still had all those bad habits.

Secondly, He wants us to make a determined choice for change. We just cannot sit there and say to God, 'Heal me.'

We have to be released from the root cause of our brokenness so that we are able to make daily choices that are no longer chained to it. It is in these choices that we are empowered to overcome the bondage that we have placed ourselves in. For if we make the right choices and see the results of applying God's Word then we know that we have the victory and this strengthens us to face future trials. As Daniel said when he faced Goliath, 'I killed a lion, I killed a bear, and this so-called giant ain't gonna destroy me.' (My paraphrase!)

New Identity

I had at last found a new identity. Previously my whole being was about being gay. I was always introduced to people with my name first followed by the statement, 'Jeff's gay'. It had become my identity; I was not a person but a label. Everything in life was attached to my being gay. My actions, motives, deeds and social life came from what I thought was my identity. I never knew myself as a son, a man, or even part of a loving family.

It is up to us to find our true identity, and out of it will come who we are and what we do. A label does not define us; it is what flows from it that makes us what we are. I am now a Christian, and it will be what flows from my life that will identify me as one. 'You were taught, with regard to your former way of life, to put off your old self, which is being corrupted by its deceitful desires; to be made new in the attitude of your minds; and to put on the new self, created to be like God in true righteousness and holiness.' (Ephesians 4:22-24)

In summary, where my Dad could not speak words of affirmation, God did (through people – for God's methodology is man); where my Dad did not spend time with me, God did (through His Spirit); what the devil intended for evil God turned around for good. Coming out of homosexuality is not easy; it has its challenges. As I mentioned earlier, if you have put years into a destructive practice it takes time to repair the damage. God has walked me through my recovery day by day, and I have learnt that there are two days I don't have to be concerned with:

yesterday and tomorrow. Yesterday is gone and we can't change the past – just the future. If I live for today, make godly choices and stay focussed on them, tomorrow will look after itself.

God wanted to restore my relationship with Him, my heavenly Father, and then with my earthly father. He asked me to deal with the issues that He brought before me and then take hold of His Word and stand on its truth. In 1997 I married my gorgeous wife. What I had thought impossible was not impossible for God. He has taken and is still taking me through the highs and lows of being restored to wholeness, of being given a life I thought I could never have; and day by day life is looking better and better.

'Jesus looked at them and said, "With man this is impossible, but with God all things are possible."' (Matthew 19:26)

CHAPTER 4

Deception: The Price Paid

'There is no such thing as a harmless lie. All deception has a cost one way or another, whether it is big or small.'
– Calvary Chapel of Sahuarita

'Do not be deceived: God cannot be mocked. A man reaps what he sows. The one who sows to please his sinful nature, from that nature will reap destruction; the one who sows to please the Spirit, from the Spirit will reap eternal life.' (Galatians 6:7,8)

In the previous chapter I told how I had lived in deception after believing a lie, the lie that I had been born gay. To think we can live in repetitive wrongdoing and not pay a price for it is also to live in deception or denial. God's word is very clear that we reap what we sow, whether for bad or for good – and in my case it was for bad. For millions of people around the world, paying the price of deception has brought so much suffering, and until the deception is broken or revealed this unwarranted suffering will continue. For many the truth has come too late, but for future generations the truth is there for the taking.

Diego Souto (musician) writes in the introductory text to the album "Palabras de Feugo" - Words of Fire, released in 1999

'Truth is more precious than lies because we cannot create the former; we can only let it express itself through us, and it is accessible to our perception in a limited way. Lies abound on our billiard-table, for these are capricious constructions. There are far more ways to miss a shot than to pot the ball.

'Why then should I wish to make the effort to uphold truth? Why should I choose to describe falsehood as a sin voluntarily entered into, rather than an excusable error? The answer is simple: I am trying to be awake in a world that invites me to dream.'

So often we allow external influences or circumstances to determine our outlook on life or our inability to succeed, using them to justify the ways we react to certain issues of life. The problem with this is that it hinders us from moving forward to accomplish our objectives or set ourselves free from bondage. In the previous chapter I explained how

God stopped me becoming a victim by taking on the responsibility for my own choices in entering the gay scene, even though the circumstances were out of my control. This 'taking on' has helped me deal with the question of why I had to be HIV positive and the issues I have had to face because of it.

I am not happy about being in this predicament – no-one is, but I have been given an inner strength to rise up against this insidious illness that has claimed so many lives over the years and is still rampant throughout the world. The drugs now on offer in some countries are preserving life for a time but still there is no cure for the virus outside of God. One thing is for sure, I will not be a victim to it, nor will I allow it to be the focus of my life. It will not control my thinking or my day-to-day living. I certainly don't live in denial that I have a virus that is trying to destroy me every day; however, I do live every day by the grace of God, and I acknowledge that He is greater than any virus, disease or health issue that the devil can throw at me.

It saddens me when I hear of those who feel HIV limits their life and who take on a victim mentality. They wouldn't need to feel that way if they could only know there is a God who is sold out to them – so much so that He gave His only Son for them (John 3:16). What has turned my thinking around since becoming a Christian is that I only have myself to blame, and in knowing that I can now accept responsibility for my own actions, take on the Word of God and get on with my life.

Accepting responsibility allows you to make the right choices to strengthen the inner man. By that I mean body, soul and spirit. I can now be everything I want to be through Christ because I live by the Word of God. I accept His word as it is.

Blame-u-titis

If I was to start blaming everybody for my life and the circumstances it has thrown at me, I might just as well roll over and die, only because life isn't over yet and there'll be a lot more stuff thrown at me before it's finished. How will I ever get strong enough to withstand the pressures of life if I just cry, 'Poor little me, the devil made me do it and it's all his fault'? The the devil didn't make me sleep around – I did. I could have a pity party and invite all my friends – *me, myself and I* – but I won't. That type of thinking takes away all the power we have to overcome the obstacles we face. It gives the devil the power to control us, and as the Word says in John 10:10, 'The thief comes only to steal and kill and destroy; I have come that they may have life, and have it to the full.'

I have told of how I had to have chemotherapy for cancer. I was starting to struggle as I approached the fourth bout of chemo, as its effects on the human body are quite radical; but 'When I am weak, He is strong'. I cried out for the mercy of God just as David did in the Psalms (too many times to list): 'May this be the last treatment, Lord, as I don't know whether I can continue.' As I sat in front of the doctor he quietly said, 'This will be your last treatment as the cancer is gone.' I have now been free of this curse for many years and am perfectly well.

The Reaping: HIV positive

A friend and I were fidgeting in the doctor's waiting room, awaiting the results of our blood tests. The doctor appeared and beckoned both of us into his room.

To my friend he said, 'Good news, you are negative.' My friend gave a deep sigh, and you could see the relief in his face. Then the doctor turned to me and said, 'Jeff, you are positive.'

My heart was beating furiously and I felt my body temperature rise. I couldn't think, I didn't know what to say. We drove home and I just sat there speechless. I walked into my bedroom, fell on the bed and cried out, 'God!

Why me?' I can still remember it so clearly today. Isn't it amazing that even when we don't know God we can still acknowledge Him in our time of need or anger?

'Do not be deceived: God cannot be mocked. A man reaps what he sows. The one who sows to please his sinful nature, from that nature will reap destruction; the one who sows to please the Spirit, from the Spirit will reap eternal life.' (Galatians 6:7-8)

It was the mid-eighties. HIV/AIDS had just begun to be the focus of world news and there was no infrastructure to deal with this virus that was starting to manifest itself. The gay community was the only 'safe' place to share with others all the fears, loneliness, sickness and death that eventually would become a tidal wave touching millions of people in literally every country in the world!

It took me weeks to come to terms with the news. I couldn't share it with anyone for some time, not even my own brother, who had also been diagnosed as HIV positive some months earlier. On top of my disillusionment with life in general I now had to contend with the fact that I had an incurable disease that was ravishing the world at an alarming rate. The newspapers were full of reports of condemnation and blame towards the gay scene for the spreading of HIV. The grim reaper advertisement was on television every day and fear was spreading through the community.

At the time I did not know of any counselling to help me deal with the grief of having a death sentence hanging over me. How does anyone deal with such news? I felt an ovewhelming sense of hopelessness, like a paper bag with all the air sucked out of it, crumpled into nothing, crunched up and thrown out in the garbage. After a little while I found the courage to share it with my brother and a few close friends. Then many of the friends around me started to share their own situations and the reality of this epidemic started to penetrate every sphere of relationship. It seemed that no-one was to be spared a premature death, that they were to be robbed of the many years of life God intended them to have.

My brother was starting to have complications on and off. I expected to have the same problems, but fortunately I was going well. I had come to know the Lord by this time and believed in a miracle not only for myself but also for my brother. Every three months I would go in for blood tests after having prayer only to find out that I was still positive. As a new Christian I just expected to be healed, but looking back I can see that God was more interested in seeing me grow into maturity as a man and working on my character than in healing my body. This may sound strange to some, but for me personally it makes sense.

'Trust in the Lord with all your heart and lean not on your own understanding; in all your ways acknowledge him, and he will make your paths straight. Do not be wise in your own eyes; fear the Lord and shun evil. This will bring health to your body and nourishment to your bones.' (Proverbs 3:5-8)

I have had the opportunity of growing strong in faith. I have always desired to be a man of faith, and if I had been healed instantly at the beginning of my walk I would not have been able to exercise my faith muscle.

'And without faith it is impossible to please God, because anyone who comes to him must believe that he exists and that he rewards those who earnestly seek him.' (Hebrews 11:6) I often think of the ten lepers whom Jesus healed as they went on their journey. What if Jesus had healed me the very first time I requested prayer? Perhaps I would not have become totally reliant on Him or trusted in Him to bring me to wholeness. I may even have slipped back into the gay scene; but it really doesn't matter now.

Soon my brother was seriously ill and confined to hospital. I was praying every day that he would be reconciled to the Father and healed. He was a man whose company I hadn't enjoyed until later in life, and now he was facing death. I didn't want to lose him, because I had learned to love him. I remember sitting in the hospice room in a corner while the family was standing beside the bed. The words of an old hymn were ringing in my head: 'Be bold, be strong for the Lord thy God is with thee.'

It got louder and louder till I responded – a bit slowly, but I was only a new Christian. I simply said, 'If it was you, Lord, take these people out of the room.' To my surprise everyone walked out. I asked for the words to say, and they were so simple. I held my brother's hand and told him how much I loved him and how much Jesus loved him. 'When you have had enough and you want to close your eyes for the last time, ask Jesus to take you home.'

Simple words – nothing fancy. This shows how passionate Christ is that none should be lost, not even homosexuals. After this the family returned to the room. There was an incredible peace and a sense of the Lord in the room. My brother responded by looking at me with drug-glazed eyes, unable to speak. I remembered a good friend telling me, 'Where there is spirit there is life,' and that God can bypass the mind and speak into the heart, for it is from there that we are judged.

He came to know the Lord, then slipped into a coma and died three days later. I believe God honoured my prayers for my bro's salvation. Then in a space of eighteen months I lost six of my friends to the same hideous illness. These were people who were made in the image of God and who, through their circumstances and brokenness, had been lost through the work of Satan.

Even though I was now a Christian, I could not ignore the price of living for many years away from God. I had to face the reality that I had reaped what I had sown. The price of deception was being paid.

CHAPTER 5

Faith Versus HIV

'Most of the important things in the world have been accomplished by people who have kept on trying when there seemed to be no hope at all.' – Dale Carnegie

Hebrews 11: 1 says, 'Now faith is being sure of what we hope for and certain of what we do not see,' and verse 6 continues, 'And without faith it is impossible to please God.' The reason I have called this chapter 'Faith versus HIV' is simply that faith in God brings life, whereas HIV without God brings death. The two can survive together, as in my case, but faith has to be the dominant and ultimate strength. Faith and HIV are on two opposing teams, and we have to decide which team we are on. We cannot spectate from midfield and believe everything will be all right, because it won't be long before the ball is passed to us and we have to make a decision which goal we will aim for, understanding that only one team will win.

To overcome the obstacles of living with HIV the first

step I had to take was to run towards the faith goal post. I did this by embracing life, and I mean to cling to it with every breath and every thought, to accept it with gladness of heart and draw into my bosom the opportunity I have been given by Christ and what He did to accomplish it.

Faith is a very personal thing. It has become part of my very being to fight against what is thrown against me, whether physical or spiritual. We must never confuse faith with presumption. Presumption can come from the mind and the heart (otherwise known as the flesh), and the Bible makes it very clear that our hearts can deceive us. We can believe a thing to be true even when it is not based on proven fact, but if we do we are relying on an unfounded assumption. The jury in a court case returns its verdict on the probability of the evidence presented to it, which is not necessarily the truth. The Word of God, however, is true and complete, making it a reliable foundation from which to make our final decisions.

For me faith comes out of the spirit, from a deep sense of the inner man and the Word of God. It is a total trust in Him to get us through the issues of life by allowing Him into those areas where we are most weak and vulnerable. We can only do this when we know who He truly is, for that gives us the confidence to step out in a way we may have struggled with previously. To have lasting faith we must believe in something or someone that has proven worthy of our trust; through the roller coaster ride of being HIV positive we need a faith that is solid and stable, a constancy from which we draw a sense of well being because we know we can rely on the object of our faith.

As I have already said, my faith is in God, 'the author and finisher of my faith'. (Hebrews 12:2) The depth of my faith in God will be determined by my knowledge and understanding of who God is and who I am in Christ. If I have a great understanding and knowledge of God, my faith will be great; if I have little knowledge, I will have little faith; if no knowledge, no faith.

The hardest part of being an HIV positive Christian has been to face the stigma attached to the virus. For many years before I became a Christian I had heard that HIV/AIDS was the judgement of God, and even more recently as a Christian I have sat in conversations where opinions freely flowed about homosexuals and those with the HIV virus.

If we believe that HIV/AIDS is the judgement of God, why don't we think the same about the flu? I think most people connect HIV/AIDS to sinful behaviour because it is a disease they can readily assign to a 'sinful' sector of society, namely homosexuals and drug addicts, and not to themselves. God did set behavioural boundaries that protect us from some diseases, but this does not change the fact that all of us have failed Him in some way. Attitudes about HIV/AIDS came from human judgement, not God's, but it nonetheless created a stigma that kept me quiet about my situation, except with very close friends, and robbed me of being true and honest about who the real Jeff was.

I was discovering that faith meant not only believing in God but trusting Him to the point of being so vulnerable in all areas of life that I felt naked.

It was nine years before I could share with my church that I had HIV. I had heard so many negative comments about it for such a long time, and fear of the virus was still very common. I recently heard that fear stands for 'false evidence appearing real'. I have found this to be true, though the Bible makes it clear that it should not be so. 'For God did not give us the spirit of fear; but of power, and of love, and of a sound mind.' (2 Timothy 1:7)

Even after HIV had been around for many years, a lot of people still did not know how they might contract the virus. Rumours were more common than truth, and it was surprising, considering all the advertising and literature available, that many had not taken the time to find out the facts.

The day came when I decided to stand before my

church family and state the truth, as doctors were giving conflicting opinions about why I had had the cancer. As I spoke people began to weep and some started praying, and when the pastors and elders gathered around me to pray, an enormous sound rushed up to Heaven as the congregation stood up and cried out to God for healing. At last the real Jeff had stood up and declared my innermost secret, allowing its darkness to leave and ushering in God's light. God's glory could not have been seen if I had continued to keep it a secret.

What it did was to bring the reality of the virus into the church, and it allowed others to follow without having to feel guilt or shame, but only the love and compassion of Christ. The testimony brought forward a myriad questions about what individuals could do to understand not only the virus but also what those infected have to deal with. I realise now that it had been an honour to have the opportunity given to me by my then-pastors Frank and Hazel Houston to be a part of tearing down Satan's stronghold – the stronghold of fear.

I had to rise above the stigma attached to being HIV positive, and that only came when I walked in confidence in who I am in Christ. To say it was easy would be lying. I had to move the knowledge from my head into my spirit, and this only came through the Word of God and time. The very first day I started courting my wife I had to confront her with the issues of having come from the gay scene and also being HIV positive. This was a daunting task, as all my life I had lived with the fear of rejection. However, the attitude I took was that if this was from God then He had already gone before me and it would work out for good. Was I apprehensive? You'd better believe it, but I wanted to be honest and up-front. After telling her, my head dropped as I waited to hear what she would say. Her reply was a simple, 'So?'

This was the second time I had experienced unconditional love. The first was when Jesus accepted me as His own, and now Lesley had accepted me also as her own. 'What shall we then say to these things? If God be for us, who can be against us?' (Romans 8:31)

A year or so back I went to a conference where God challenged me in the area of faith. I had gone to the meetings with my own agenda, but God also had His. On the last day of the conference His agenda met mine.

What God put to me was that I had trusted Him in many areas of my life. However, if I was to move into a higher level of faith for the next season of my life, I had to step out and give up my dependence on the medications I was taking and replace them with Him. After much prayer and discussion with my wife, we both agreed I would do it.

Now, I want to make it very clear that this is not for everyone who is believing for God to move. If you are on any medication for whatever illness, do not stop it. This is where faith and presumption have to be very clearly defined. Everyone has a different walk, and God deals with everyone differently.

If I had not firmly believed God had spoken to me I would not have stopped medication. However, I was confident that He was answering my prayers and taking me to task on it. In my early years as a Christian God gave me a scripture to take hold of: 'I will not die but live, and will proclaim what the Lord has done. The Lord has chastened me severely, but he has not given me over to death.' (Psalm 118:17-18)

Now, you might be thinking that if God has told you you won't die of an HIV-related illness you don't need to be walking in faith. *Wrong!* It has always been up to me to exercise the faith I have. I am seeking total healing, so I still have to walk the walk,

> *'My obligation is to do the right thing. The rest is in God's hands.'*
> – Martin Luther King Jr.

talk the talk, live by faith and do the right thing, for I am seeking something that is impossible for me to achieve. I have had to trust God by applying His Word, for then and only then does it become powerful. Once again it comes back to choice: we can either receive or reject God's Word and what He might be saying to us.

Faith is something we have to exercise in order to get what we ask; it is an active part of Christian living. In the Scriptures we find a number of conditions for God to act in our lives, reminders of our responsibility to obey. They are expressed by words like 'do', 'if you' and 'keep' in Exodus 15:26: *'If you* listen carefully to the voice of the Lord your God and *do* what is right in his eyes, *if you* pay attention to his commands and *keep* all his decrees, I will not bring on you any of the diseases I brought on the Egyptians, for I am the Lord, who heals you.'

When you are patiently trusting God for a miracle you can feel profoundly alone. Unless you have been in this situation it can be difficult to understand: any little cough or feeling of being unwell, even if totally unrelated to your sickness, can be a reminder of the situation you are in and fill your mind with anxiety.

Thankfully Jesus said, 'I will never leave you, nor forsake you'.

CHAPTER 6

Fight or Failure

'We shall not flag or fail. We shall go on to the end. We shall fight in France, we shall fight on the seas and oceans, we shall fight with growing confidence and growing strength in the air; we shall defend our island, whatever the cost may be. We shall fight on the beaches, we shall fight on the landing grounds, we shall fight in the fields and in the streets, we shall fight in the hills; we shall never surrender.'
– Winston Churchill

Winston Churchill acknowledged he had a crisis on his hands. He knew that to win each battle and end the war triumphant he had to pitch Britain's depleted forces onto the offensive while also resisting the enemy's attacks on all fronts.

Being HIV positive in a negative world means being under attack, too, and I have learnt an important lesson: if I am to beat this attack that wars against my body daily, I have to fight. No war can be won from the sidelines expecting someone else to do the work. The battle is the Lord's *and* mine.

In the previous chapters I have mentioned many times the power of choice and responsibility and the results of exercising it. Being the man God has called me to be, as well as being the husband my wife believes in and loves, empowers me to make choices and take on the responsibility to live life to the fullest as I wait on the Lord. My role as a husband and leader of the home requires me to be strong, to be a provider in all areas of life and weather the storms that so often come to try us. Even though my wife is aware that God could take me (or either of us) at any time He wants, it is up to me to ensure that God's purposes for our lives, as individuals and as a married couple, are fulfilled. It is my duty to fight the war that rages on the inside as a result of being HIV positive as well as the spiritual war that we all face daily.

When I recited my wedding vows and said 'through better and through worse', I took on the obligation to do whatever it takes to see the marriage through to the end and not allow HIV to destroy what God was building, regardless of the opposition. It comes back to my choice as to whether I want to fight or fail.

However, there are times when our walk with God can

be like a roller coaster ride. We soar like an eagle, then plummet like a turkey. Our emotions become so unstable that they throw our faith around like a tornado. I know – I've been there. God revealed to me some ways of keeping stability in my life as I wait upon him, and they have brought me peace. Let's look at the woman with the issue of blood in Mark 5: 25-34.

There were some factors in her life that brought about her healing. I find this passage one of the Bible's most inspiring, as it speaks of life, love and hope for those suffering with any illness, whether physical or emotional. It speaks of a God who has authority over death and disease and who will stop and respond to you.

1. Persistence

Verse 26: 'She had suffered a great deal under the care of many doctors and had spent all she had, yet instead of getting better she grew worse.'

Persistence means standing firm in the face of opposition – and she had it. She faced opposition physically and financially having spent all her money on doctors. Her appearance must have been ghastly after losing blood for twelve years. Even the Levitical (Jewish) law was against her, branding her as unclean and perhaps even obliging her to cry out 'Unclean!' as she walked around. Everything seemed to be against her. However, she intended to be a victor, not a victim.

She wasn't an oppositionist but an opportunist. She grasped every opportunity she could to reach her goal – to be healed. Her desire for healing was greater than any opposition or pain, whether of ostracism, rejection or physical suffering, that she had to face.

> *'There is no security on this earth, there is only opportunity.'*
> - General Douglas MacArthur

Persistence is probably the most important quality for success in achieving our daily goals. The degree of persistence we have will determine the level of our desire to reach a goal. It is the key that can unlock the chains that have prevented our success in the past. Persistence can help us develop the mindset we need to hurdle the obstacles that life will throw against us. When you are facing a life-threatening disease the challenges are not only spiritual and physical, they can also come from those around you who do not understand your faith and determination. Often enough they will come through negative speaking, which I will deal with further on.

How do we stay motivated enough to keep persisting

through trials? I believe the key is to keep the end in mind. For example, if your goal is healing, focus on the healing. If you focus on the end you will find it much easier to work through the steps that will get you there.

Over a hundred years ago there was a man who had a dream of building a horseless carriage that was affordable and family oriented. For almost twenty years he faced bankruptcy several times over as well as disappointment, ridicule and failure, but he didn't give up. His name was Henry Ford – and the rest is history.

Martin Luther King Jr had a dream, and we all know it well. His dream may have cost him his life but the legacy of that dream impacted millions of lives worldwide and is still outworking itself to this day. Your dream might have a greater impact on others than you realise – only God knows that, and perhaps if only for this reason we should persist. We can probably all name great people in history who achieved great things only because they persisted through years of disappointment.

2. Positioning

Verse 27: 'When she heard about Jesus…'

To be positioned is to be in an occupied place or fortified place. Fortified means to be strengthened against attack.

We often hear of someone being 'in the right place at the right time' to get a job or some other benefit. We think such things happen by chance, but in reality it is God's purpose for us to be in the proper place at each stage of our lives. When we are in the right place or the right situation it allows God to release His supernatural supply to sustain us throughout difficult times. In 1 Kings 17 God tells Elijah to go to the Brook Cherith after prophesying famine to King Ahab. Elijah did what God instructed and throughout the famine God supernaturally supplied food through ravens. If Elijah had disobeyed God and gone elsewhere he would have starved and missed out on the divine supply of God. In Exodus 40 Moses received instructions from God to build the tabernacle and put everything in its right place, and in verses 33-34 we see that when Moses had finished the task the glory of God filled the place. When we, like the woman with the issue of blood, are in the right place we not only receive divine supply for our lives but we are also consumed by the glory of God.

So how did this woman who was seeking her miracle know about Jesus? I believe she had been in places where she had heard about the many miracles He had performed and it had built her faith – places like church or other surroundings that glorify God, that release His glory,

His provision and His protection and build the faith that strengthens us against the enemy's attacks when he tries to rob us of our faith, our dreams, our healing and our hopes.

'Then faith comes by hearing, and hearing by the word of God.' (Romans 10:17)

3. Perception

To be perceptive means to have sensitive insight into a person or a situation, to look through the way things appear and gain knowledge about what is happening beyond the purely physical realm.

But knowledge is not what brings about change; what counts is the application of that knowledge. Once she knew about Jesus the woman went further and took hold of the promises of God to the point that she pursued Him and reached out to Him. She applied what she had heard about Him and only then saw the Word of God in action. 'For the Word of God is living and active. Sharper than any double-edged sword, it penetrates even to dividing soul and spirit, joints and marrow; it judges the thoughts and attitudes of the heart.' (Hebrews 4:12)

This woman's perception of Jesus had come from firstly being in the right place to gather information about Him and then using that information to understand what He meant to her personally. Her perception about Christ was to understand His value – the revelation of truth – which then protected her from falling victim to lies and deception.

Conversely, we can see why listening to gossip is so damaging, and how judging others on false information warps our perception of them. The broken relationships that result from such judgement rob both parties of fellowship for no good reason.

4. Pursuit

Verse 27: 'She came up behind him in the crowd and touched his cloak…'

To engage in pursuit is to act on a desire to make an effect or accomplish an end, to strive to overtake or capture an object. This takes effort and discipline. As Christians we have to examine our hearts: are we truly pursuing God or just acknowledging Him? We often put great effort into pursuing our dreams while only passively acknowledging the One who provides them. The truth is, we cannot pursue something we are not seeking.

'But seek first the kingdom of God, and his righteousness; and all these things shall be added unto you.' (Matthew 6:33)

Usually we only pursue something if we see good

reason for it. This woman had a goal or an objective to pursue Christ, and we know it was healing. Purpose is a drive that propels or motivates us to achieve our desired goals and find meaning in our lives. We all have a purpose for being on this planet – a purpose that God has entrusted to us not only to discover but also to fulfil.

> *'Life without purpose is an experiment'*
> – Tim Storey

5. Positive Confession

Verse 28: 'For she said, If I may but touch his clothes, I shall be well.'

To have a positive confession is to have absolutely no doubt – not to even question, but simply to speak and believe. Because she had been positioned to hear the Word of God, the woman was perceptive and able to speak positively.

'Reckless words pierce like a sword, but the tongue of the wise brings healing.' (Proverbs 12:18)

Words are the most powerful things in the world. Saying we can or cannot do something usually determines if we will achieve it or not. Earlier I mentioned that saying 'I have to' or 'I choose to' can determine whether or not we are set free from bondages. The same can be said for positive or negative speaking. Many of us have become captive to our own words, even in prayer, which have stopped us receiving from God. We pray the problem and receive it. Have you ever cried out, 'God, I'm not healed yet,' or 'The prayer didn't work'? Whoops!

'Therefore I tell you, whatever you ask for in prayer, believe that you have received it, and it will be yours.' (Mark 11:24)

When God brought everything into being He did it by the spoken word. If the spiritual world is controlled by the Word of God, the natural world is to be controlled by the tongue of man, which was meant to speak God's word. Many of us, including myself, never understood that all words spoken are implementing a spiritual law and we will reap what we sow. I speak to my body and my immune system with words of healing because I have come to know the power of the words that flow from my mouth. When I speak health and the written word of God I am bringing God into the picture; however, if I speak negativity I am bringing the devil in, and he only brings death and destruction.

We must remove ourselves from negative surroundings. The devil can use them to destroy our very hope, and as we live in a negative world we need to stand against it, positioning ourselves where hope lives. I have learnt to walk away from negativity as God makes it clear to me what negative or complaining people can do:

'How long will this wicked community grumble against me? I have heard the complaints of these grumbling Israelites. So tell them, "As surely as I live, declares the LORD, I will do to you the very things I heard you say."' (Numbers 14:27-28)

In church or amongst our brothers and sisters we often speak our 'Christianese' jargon, but what do we speak outside the church when we are facing struggles on our own and no-one but God can hear us? Do we speak words of praise for our Lord and Saviour, expressing our faith and hope in Him, or do we speak out words of doubt and negativity?

I never knew how negative I was until I started courting my wife. We were out driving one day and I made a comment. She replied sharply, 'Don't be so negative.' It wasn't until she repeated what I had said that I realised she was correct. Here I was – Mr Negative himself. It made me think about the words that had been spoken in my family for all those years, and I realised I came from a negative-speaking family. I had to re-learn my whole way of speaking and learn to think before I opened my mouth. Ask people to correct you if they hear you speaking negatively! You need to be speaking words of life and encouragement that will manifest in your life. Remember – you reap what you sow!

6. Proclamation

Verse 33: 'But the woman fearing and trembling, knowing what was done in her, came and fell down before him, and *told him all the truth.*'

This was simply the power of confession. When the power of words are married to the truth, it speaks life and hope. She acknowledged that when she touched Him she was healed, and so she gave praise where it was deserved.

'But in your hearts set apart Christ as Lord. Always be prepared to give an answer to everyone who asks you to give the reason for the hope that you have. But do this with gentleness and respect.' (1 Peter 3:15)

'And hope does not disappoint us, because God has poured out his love into our hearts by the Holy Spirit, whom he has given us.' (Romans 5:5)

The woman's persistence, positioning, pursuit, positive confession and proclamation gave her peace.

7. Peace

Verse 34: 'And He said to her, "Daughter, your faith has made you well. Go in peace and be healed of your affliction."'

God gave the woman more than she was looking for – and so it is with all of us who are suffering in some way.

Our heavenly Dad is not one to hold anything back from us unless it might hinder us. No wise dad will ever give gifts that might endanger or ensnare his children, and God is a generous Dad who desires nothing but the best for us. It is true that it is all in His timing and something that we must never forget is that He sees the complete picture from beginning to end.

I have peace in life whether or not I am HIV positive simply because my hope for all things is not in myself or in man but in Christ.

'Which of you, if his son asks for bread, will give him a stone? Or if he asks for a fish, will give him a snake? If you, then, though you are evil, know how to give good gifts to your children, how much more will your Father in heaven give good gifts to those who ask him!' (Matthew 7:9-11)

Even though God gave me Psalm 118:17-18 to hold on to, it is my responsibility to walk it into being. I could have rejected it all, and therefore negated His promises, but I chose to receive.

I share this with you so as to give you hope for a miracle if you need one, or for you to find the God of all hope who is waiting for you to touch the hem of His garment.

This woman had to push through the crowd, and so may you. Let me say to you that God wants to give you more than you might ask for. She was reaching out for the compassion and mercy of the Most High God and He gave her healing, salvation and peace for the rest of her life. If you live with Him you might have opposition to face and challenges to overcome – but isn't it worth the effort?

CHAPTER 7

Life with Lesley

'He who finds a wife finds what is good and receives favour from the LORD.' – Proverbs 18:22

One thing I can say from experience is that once God starts working in your life He never stops. His love is too great to leave you where you are; He takes you on a journey alongside Him, moving you from glory to glory.

To leave my wife out of this testimony would be like leaving Jesus out of the Bible. Lesley has been an integral part of my journey to the man I am today. She has been used by God to help develop my manhood and to teach me the art of communicating, not just as a man to a woman but also as a husband. I never knew how to communicate with women intimately because I never had a role model to learn from and I never had a need or desire to. My focus and interest had been predominantly towards the male – yet now here I am enjoying marriage and the life God has given back to me!

It has not been easy, for to start learning about the opposite sex at the age of forty and over is a huge task for anyone. I remember starting Bible college and having to do an assignment within the first few weeks. I had not been to school for decades, and I had to do an assignment? I freaked out, and it was the same when God introduced Lesley into my life. But what was different was the stirring within me, desiring the companionship not just of a woman but specifically of her. My life had been like an unassembled jigsaw puzzle with fragmented pieces scattered all over the place, but then, finally, God started to put the pieces together. Lesley, however, was the crucial piece that brought completion to God's master plan of restoration.

The previous seven years had been a time of dealing with the internal issues of my brokenness and preparing to turn them around and bring them to wholeness. (Though in saying this, we know that complete wholeness won't be achieved until Christ returns.)

I was working in a small office in the church, looking after the administration of a ministry that dealt with sexual brokenness, when Lesley blew in like a hurricane asking to see the leader. After I explained that he was not in she blew out again. I remember thinking how attractive she was, but never in my wildest dreams could I have imagined what was to unfold over time. We bumped into each other from time to time, but when I was in Bible college a year or so later we saw more of each other. I felt encouraged to invite her out for the occasional coffee and just get to know her. This became a regular occurrence, but it was not until I went for a holiday to Fiji that I discovered I was obsessed with her. When I found myself sending postcards and telephoning her regularly I became quite perturbed, but also excited. What was happening? My Fijian friends who knew me for my past lifestyle could not understand it, either, and were quite amused.

On my return to Sydney I went back to college and asked her to be my girlfriend. I felt like a fifteen-year-old kid, but I knew that God had started something very special and I wanted to go along with it. As I've said, she accepted me and my past and all that went along with it. This was one truly amazing woman, and I knew then that she would be my wife – but I had to trust God and gather the courage to ask her. I felt like Joshua crossing the River Jordan to take hold of the land God was giving the children of Israel.

'Have I not commanded you? Be strong and courageous. Do not be terrified; do not be discouraged, for the LORD your God will be with you wherever you go.' (Joshua 1:9)

When we announced our engagement there were

those who felt it was wrong for her to marry someone who had come out from the gay scene. There was one person who released the information that I was HIV positive, not directly to her but to another person, knowing it would get back to her. We both knew our marriage was from God and no man was going to stop it. This is why it had been so important to tell her right from the start about all my faults and failings, as it negated what the enemy was trying to do.

As she walked down the isle I was totally blown away by her beauty and by the way God had given this treasure to me. There is something very special about a woman of God on her wedding day. I was overwhelmed with it all, and I stood in amazement to think that after all those years of wanting to be married and live a life of normality it was now coming to pass. As she moved closer towards me all my insecurities rose up before me again and all the old questions came flooding back: 'Are you sure, God? What if I didn't hear from you? What if I'm wrong?' At the end of the service we shared our first kiss. Yes, our first kiss! All the time we were courting I never kissed her, as this woman deserved respect and honour. I never wanted her to feel that I was taking advantage of her in any way, and I believe this was from God to enable her to build trust in me.

Lesley has stood beside me through all the highs and

lows, particularly when the cancer hit and when I struggled through the issues God placed in front of me. It could be said that you can be male, a man and a husband, but I have found that they are three different components. They each have their own challenges, but somehow God brings them together into oneness to bring glory to Him and happiness to the wife.

I still have a long way to go, but now I don't feel I am on my own. Just like all men, I have had to learn what it is to be a man *and* to be a husband. It doesn't come naturally, and with learning come mistakes.

Throughout my old lifestyle I had been the follower, the person who just agreed with whoever I was with just to keep the peace. Every time I did this it only confirmed the sense of uselessness in me and made me totally unhappy. I never felt strong enough to stand up for what I believed, and would never confront another person for fear of being ridiculed and rejected. In reality I was being totally dominated and controlled and felt my thoughts were not worth considering. It was a major step in losing my identity; it stripped me of my right to become my own person – and yet, in saying this, I had made my own choice to allow it to happen.

Nonetheless, here I am now, a married man finding out what it is to be a man and a husband. Being a husband is not only a privileged role that is not to be taken for granted, it is also a role brimming with the challenges of being a man. As head of the house I am responsible for my wife's spiritual walk and the provider not only of the finances but also of the direction we are to take with God. I need to be fully aware of my wife's emotional needs and provide a ready ear for her when I fail – not just so she can rebuke me, but so I can become more sensitive to her needs and learn to meet them. For me this is a paradigm shift in thinking, but what it has done is to force me to draw on the strength I had when I entered the marriage and keep exercising it like a muscle. The object of this is to help me grow in confidence in decision making, because in the end I will be accountable to God for what He has entrusted to me. I am learning that if both of us focus on the other's needs, emotionally, physically and spiritually, then both of us will be filled, as the focus will be directed outwards towards each other, not inwards into ourselves. Selfishness starves the soul of a marriage.

Since I never had a role model to show me what a husband should be, I have observed married men whom I respect and taken a lead from them. I have allowed these men of God to be my role models, as I firmly believe it is never too late to learn, and God has put them around me for a reason.

Being a keep-the-peace guy meant avoiding arguments and therefore never learning to resolve conflicts. This, then, has been a major learning curve for me in marriage. I have had to overcome the sense that my opinions were worthless and learn that I am a person of value, a man my wife loves, that she cares about how I am feeling and I can allow her into my emotions.

I have finally come to acknowledge that differences are valid and that we need to resolve them, not avoid them. This is a totally new concept for me, but I am determined to break through with it, for every issue I have to deal with is crucial in my development as a man.

I have found there is a sense of fulfilment in marriage, an awareness of completion as a person. As husband and wife we share dreams that are intertwined for a purpose, not only in serving God but also in growing together as a team. I am learning about football, Lesley is learning about motor racing. Why? It is part of growing together and expanding the sphere of our relationship. Taking an interest in your partner's enjoyments is a part of giving yourself to him or her.

Six months after being married and one month out of Bible college we were sent off on a missionary trip to the mountains of Sri Lanka. Totally inexperienced as a missionary and as a husband, I was told we were going to pastor English speaking nationals in a small church. However, when we arrived we found out the church had split, so we had to restore unity and bring back those who had left. This was a big challenge for us both, and being newly married I quickly had to learn how to place boundaries around our marriage, constantly remind myself I was not a single man any more and, most importantly, include my wife in all things.

Throughout this time my wife was a tower of strength and support for me. I know it was very difficult for her but she stood firm in God even through the tears when I rejected her guidance in an immature way. To think I had made her cry grieved me intensely, but I learnt very quickly that giving advice was her way of showing me love. After living with rejection for so many years, here was someone who truly, unconditionally loved me; yet I have found it very difficult to learn to receive love. Lesley has persisted in teaching me how to accept a compliment at times when I had such a poor view of myself. It is interesting to note that many of us can receive ridicule or negativity so easily but find it very difficult to accept anything encouraging or positive.

After seven months we arrived back in Sydney having learnt some very significant lessons from all areas of life and having many stories to tell. We had seen lives reconciled to God, many people come back to church, bombs explode near our home – we experienced a lot of things in that short space of time.

While we were there we inherited our dog Lady. We fell in love with her the very first day she was given to us, and she was definitely a Godsend for Lesley. We saw Lady give birth to ten puppies that we named after ten pastors we knew, according to their personalities. When Lady picked up poison laid down by farmers, God provided a miracle of assistance, and to this day we stand in awe of how God did this for our dog.

When we were due to return to Australia no-one believed we would be able to bring her with us – in fact, we were told emphatically that it would be impossible to get her into the country. However, God kept telling me to encourage Lesley with the words, 'Where there's a will, there's a way,' and we based our prayers on these very words. We had the will and God had the way, and the thought of leaving her and saying good-bye wrenched our hearts. Yes, mine too – I was softening!

That amazing dog, that would sit every Sunday on the front row of the church alongside Lesley listening to my inexperienced preaching, arrived in Australia six months after we did, having flown from Sri Lanka, holidayed at a boarding kennel in Los Angeles and stopped over in Singapore on the way. When tensions were high God used Lady to bring us peace and teach me never to let situations or circumstances get in the way of love. Animals can teach us so much about faithfulness and unconditional love if we are open to be taught. She is our daughter, our gift from God, who constantly reminds me of His faithfulness to what was a very broken person and how He overcomes the impossible.

Life with Lesley is a gift from God of immeasurable proportion. Nothing could compare to this blessed opportunity of being her husband and this foundation motivates me to work on the issues that God places in front of me even when I just want to grumble. Many men could say that about their wives, but this is my book and my own special story. After all, how many women could receive a man who has come from the gay scene and is HIV positive? They are certainly not in the majority!

God saved the best till last and He gave her to me.

CHAPTER 8

Things I've Learnt

'There are three principal means of acquiring knowledge... observation of nature, reflection, and experimentation. Observation collects facts; reflection combines them; experimentation verifies the result of that combination.'
– Denis Diderot

The truth was that all through my old lifestyle I firmly believed God hated homosexuals, that we were all condemned to hell and were a group who bore the brunt of jokes and ridicule. Ministers of the gospel would speak against homosexuals, and I particularly remember seeing a picture in an overseas magazine of Christians carrying placards saying 'God hates faggots'.

Never do I remember hearing words of love or acceptance of us as created beings made in the image of God. As some people don't understand what the word 'image' means, I will explain: an image is something that is the same as, or has a likeness to, an original. God has a mind, a will and emotions like those He has given us. However, He was exempt from the Fall, and we must never forget the impact the Fall had on humanity. If we keep this in mind it enables us to have a greater understanding of brokenness, which will, hopefully, help us not to be so judgmental.

Nowhere in the Bible can I find God condemning a person for being a person. He condemned the behaviour or actions or motives of people but not the emotional side of that person. So if God had this hatred for homosexuals that I had heard so much about, why did He save me? Why has God taken me and many others from the gay scene, turned our lives around and taken us from glory to glory to preach the unsearchable riches of Christ? I believe it can be summed up in three words: love, grace and mercy. He understands the brokenness of humanity like no-one else can, and He grieves over it.

John Stott writes in *Same Sex Partners?*, 'The attitude of personal antipathy towards homosexuals is nowadays termed "homophobia". It is a mixture of irrational fear, hostility and even revulsion. It overlooks that fact that the majority of homosexual people are probably not responsible for their condition (though they are, of course, for their conduct).'

He then goes on to say, 'At the heart of the homosexual condition is a deep loneliness, the natural human hunger for mutual love, a search for identity, and a longing for completeness. If homosexual people cannot find these things in the local "church family", we have no business to go on using that expression.'

Some years ago I was outside a building in the centre of the gay community in Sydney. A ministry I was involved with at the time was having an outreach, and I was waiting for the other members of the team to arrive. I noticed a young man walking towards me, and suddenly I began to weep. I had no control over it; I felt grieved, and it increased the closer this young man came toward me. I couldn't turn away, but I just had to bear it as he walked past. God said to me, 'This young man is going to hand over his body to another man tonight as an act of love.' I believe God gave me His eyes for that moment in time. I felt His heart being broken as this man went on his way. After he had passed I made my way into the building, but then another type of grief hit me as I realised I had missed an opportunity of planting a seed of love, grace and mercy into that young man's life. No Bible-bashing, no condemnation, no judgmental words – just love, grace and mercy.

So, then, after writing all this I come back to the question, 'Why, God, why did you choose me?'

The fact is, He has chosen all of us who have a story to tell of a faithful God who took our brokenness upon Himself on the cross and imparts wholeness when we seek Him and respond to Him: 'Then you will call upon me and come and pray to me, and I will listen to you. You will seek me and find me when you seek me with all your heart.' (Jeremiah 29:12-13)

Then comes His promise – and this is the exciting part: '"I will be found by you," declares the LORD, "and will bring you back from captivity…"' (Jeremiah 29:14)

Isn't that incredible! God, the Creator of the entire world, the same God who put all the stars in heaven, who put the universe in its place, will find us (you) and bring us (you) out of the brokenness that has held us (yes, *you*!) captive and placed us in bondage to sin.

But it goes even further than that. God's heart is also to give you a life you had never imagined, a life of peace and fulfilment – perhaps a life you did once dream about, as I did for many years. Make no mistake: God is passionate about making you the man or woman He meant you to be from the beginning of time.

Why would He do all this? John 3:16 says, 'For God so

loved the world that he gave his one and only Son, that whoever believes in him shall not perish but have eternal life.'

Love – the very thing many of us were seeking, though our search had led us into a lifestyle God never intended. The devil – the killer, thief and destroyer – had fooled many people, me included, into feeling void of the very thing that gives life. However, God understood this and returned it to us through His Son. *His* love is a love that our finite minds cannot fathom. It is more profound than we could ever imagine and meets the very need that lies deepest in our hearts.

'But God chose the foolish things of the world to shame the wise; God chose the weak things of the world to shame the strong.' – 1 Corinthians 1:27-29

Many of us like to see ourselves as wise. We don't like to be called foolish or weak, but the truth is that for myself I was foolish and my life showed it: bad choices brought forth bad fruit. Sure, I had material possessions, but they didn't bring me peace and contentment and they couldn't give me stability while I was in ungodly relationships. I was foolish, weak and lowly, and certainly despised by many.

> *It wasn't until quite late in life that I discovered how easy it is to say, 'I don't know'.*
>
> – W Somerset Maugham

I felt I was a 'nothing' in this world.

Now I have wisdom – God's wisdom. I have strength – His strength. I have acceptance because of Jesus and I am a 'something'. I am a child of the Most High God and a husband, not a has-been. What is the fruit of your life? What are you producing, remembering that like produces like? Are you producing joy, peace and happiness from your choices in life? Do you have a contentment that is on solid ground, or does it sway whenever a challenge comes before you?

To be strong, to be wise, is to acknowledge that you don't have all the answers. To make yourself vulnerable to the fact that you may be living a lie or in deception is strength. To ask God to reveal the truth to you and give you the courage to face it is wisdom.

It was pride that changed angels into devils; it is humility that makes men as angels. – Saint Augustine

Pride can be a good thing, as when parents are proud of their children and I am proud of my wife. However, we can take pride and turn it into arrogance, which leaves us open to defeat and pain. Therefore it is as well for me to remember that everything my wife has become is because of God and that it was God who took me, a lowly and weak thing, and turned me into a person of worth. I acknowledge that He has done this so that I can stay humble, leave pride at the door, and give Him all the praise.

Humility is one of the world's best kept secrets. 'He chose the lowly things of this world and the despised things – and the things that are not – to nullify the things that are so that no one may boast before him.' (1 Corinthians 1:27-29)

Hope in God

'Command those who are rich in this present world not to be arrogant nor to put their hope in wealth, which is so uncertain, but to put their hope in God, who richly provides us with everything for our enjoyment.' (1 Timothy 6:17)

If we were to be honest with ourselves, we would all be hoping for something of special significance to happen in our lives, perhaps a dream to come to fruition or that particular job you've been searching for, that healing, that special person to walk into your life… True?

Hope is *that special something* we desire, accompanied by an expectation that the thing we want will happen.

Hope is the foundation for that happening.

When I received Christ as my Lord and Saviour I had an inner hope of not only having my sexual identity changed but also of being healed of HIV. The hope was just there. It is something you cannot easily explain, but you know it is real. It lies in the core of the soul, and the only way to remove it is to go back to a previous way of life that offered no hope.

'And hope does not disappoint us, because God has poured out his love into our hearts by the Holy Spirit, whom he has given us.' (Romans 5:5)

So the hope I have results from the love of God. I have many dreams that I hope will come to pass, but if I put my hope in myself or in other people I am relying on someone who is human and fragile and has plenty of their own issues to deal with! Are other people really any different from me? Of course not! We know they have their faults and failings, and yet we often get so disappointed when they let us down. I am hoping to become more and more a man according to God, a better husband, a soul winner and many other things God intends for me. However, I'm not putting my hope in man but in God, for the things I'm seeking are not under human control. He may use men or women to teach, encourage, challenge or even rebuke me, but the change will come as I seek God and trust that He will provide all that is needed – as it will for you, too.

Trust in God

'Do not let your hearts be troubled. Trust in God; trust also in me.' (1 John 14:1, Jesus speaking)

Now that I have learned to put all my hope in God, I have to learn to trust Him. That is a big ask for anyone who has been disappointed many times, as we all have in one way or another. When we have experienced many let-downs from our own dads, how do we learn to trust our heavenly Father?

Trust, says the New Oxford Dictionary, is a 'firm belief in the reliability, truth, ability or strength of someone or something'. The inference is that the person or thing has integrity and possesses a quality or attribute that inspires confidence. To anyone who finds it difficult to trust, let me say I understand: I know it takes time. When I was first saved I didn't trust anyone. I found it difficult to be hugged, as previously I had been hugged for the wrong reasons. It comes back to being discerning about when to make yourself vulnerable and allowing God to change your perception and mindset. A child learns to walk with their parents' arms there ready to catch them, and our heavenly Dad is like that.

As a child I was promised many things, yet the promises fell on barren ground. I can therefore understand the difficulty some may have in trusting our heavenly Dad. I can only say that for my part I have found Him faithful and worthy of all the trust and hope we give Him.

"'For my thoughts are not your thoughts, neither are your ways my ways," declares the LORD. "As the heavens are higher than the earth, so are my ways higher than your ways and my thoughts than your thoughts.'" (Isaiah 55:8-9)

> *'Change and growth take place when a person has risked himself and dares to become involved with experimenting with his own life.'*
> – Herbert Otto

When I left the gay scene – and I'm sure the same applies for any lifestyle – I found that when I put my hope and trust in God He worked things out His way. Trying to understand what is happening is normal, but it can be very frustrating, for you will discover that God often does the reverse to what our human minds would expect. This is where we have to trust Him and just let God be God. 'Be still, and know that I am God…' (Psalm 46:10) Remember to be humble and take on godly wisdom; trust, hope and watch your life change.

'Trust in the LORD with all your heart and lean not on your own understanding; in all your ways acknowledge him, and he will make your paths straight. Do not be wise in your own eyes; fear the LORD and shun evil. This will bring health to your body and nourishment to your bones.' (Proverbs 3:5-8)

Continuance of Faith

'Now faith is the substance of things hoped for, the evidence of things not seen.' (Hebrews 11:1)

Over the centuries we have read about mighty men and women of faith who have accomplished great feats. We have put some of them on pedestals, for although they were only ordinary people like you and me they had a quality that placed them above many others and landed some of them in the history books. What was the particular quality that distinguished them? I believe it was their determination never to give up on what they believed or desired. I sit in church every week and see people who, just like those we read about, are seeking something from God and who have a determination that never gives up. They are the ones who inspire me to persevere in seeking what is impossible for man, just like the woman with the issue of blood in Mark's gospel.

I have watched a woman who, over the years, believed God for a miracle to make her walk again. I saw her progress from a wheelchair to crutches, and now she walks without assistance. Her determination and faith in God have given her what she sought and desired because she didn't give up. It was a walk of faith that through time and determination resulted in a miracle. This is inspirational stuff that can only come to fruition through God. Yet through all of her prayers she just believed and had hope in something she could not see. I can look back and see that through her walk she applied the principles I mentioned earlier about the woman with the issue of blood: persistence, positioning, perception, pursuing God, positive confession and proclamation. This built her faith, and her perseverance brought her to the point where she could walk normally.

Some see Job as the most depressing book in the Bible, and to a degree I can understand them. But let's look beyond the fact the he lost everything, including his family. When he was being persecuted by his so-called friends (and his wife), being told to confess sin and curse God, Job would not. He held on to the belief that God was good, and trusted in the God of the impossible. Job was honoured for his faith, and God restored everything he had lost and much more besides.

I remember returning to my doctor for a blood test result. My faith was high and as usual I had believed for a miracle report. The doctor delivered the results and I was disappointed that my T-cell reading was not what I had believed for. I allowed my faith to fall and took on a wounded spirit. By that time I had been a Christian for many years and I should have known better than to do that, but I did and it took me weeks to rise above it and start building my faith again. The devil will try and rob us of every bit of faith and hope – so be on guard!

'Be self-controlled and alert. Your enemy the devil prowls around like a roaring lion looking for someone to devour.' (1 Peter 5:8)

Three months later I received my next blood test result, and it was no better. In the meantime, however, I had learnt a huge lesson, so I picked up the report, read it and praised God for my life and all that He had done. Whose report was I going to believe? The Lord's report, of course! Though it is easy to say that now, at the time it was anything but easy. Yet once I had praised God I was filled with an incredible joy, and I rejoiced in Him all the way home. I voiced the praises of the Lord in words and song, and it took me to a new level of faith that has only grown in the years since then. Even as a Christian I have made mistakes, like the one I just mentioned, but through my mistakes have come some of my greatest victories.

You may be seeking a miracle for healing, you may be coming out of a lifestyle that has left you scarred, you may be struggling with identity issues, whether sexual, relational or whatever. Let me advise you as one who has done it: place yourself around people who inspire you, who have been there and persevered until they triumphed. For me, perseverance is not an option but has become an integral characteristic of my lifestyle.

CHAPTER 9

Walking Out a Miracle

'There are no miracles for those who have no faith in them.' – French proverb

I would love to explain why God doesn't go around dispensing instant miracles, but unfortunately I can't. I'm sure there are those who can – some people have an answer for everything! – but I've come to the conclusion that how God works is God's business and that's that. So, having settled that, I can now focus on the things God wants me to focus on, and this gives me peace. I can see why God wanted me to work through the issues of my old lifestyle and my recovery and didn't just miraculously make me whole. The truth is, of course, even those of us who seem whole are still broken to some degree and it is a lifetime's walk to repair past hurts.

What I am saying here is that if you need a miracle – and most of us do at times – then focus on what God is saying to you and leave the worrying to Him. He knows what you need better than anyone. It doesn't mean you stop praying or believing for it, just don't let it obsess you. If HIV and my healing had consumed me, I would have become a very disillusioned and disappointed man. If I hadn't had faith-filled people around me at that time I might even have turned away from God.

I still seek God for my healing and I'm not going to let Him forget about it! I also have many people praying for me, but in the meantime I'm getting on with what God has called me to do. That, my friends, is a learning curve: I have learnt not to question God about it but to take in what He is telling me. *He*, not the problem, is the focus, and *He* is the provider of the solution.

The Power of Purpose

What God has done in my life is a miracle, and this is the absolute truth. With the miracle of transformation has come a sense of purpose, and this purpose has given meaning to my life. It has given me a desire to achieve my life's goals and a hunger for the things of God. All of us need to know, even as children, that we are important and that our lives have meaning.

Purpose is the resolve with which we steel ourselves to accomplish a desired result. 'Therefore, since we are surrounded by such a great cloud of witnesses, let us throw off everything that hinders and the sin that so easily entangles, and let us run with perseverance the race marked out for us. Let us fix our eyes on Jesus, the author and perfecter of our faith, who for the joy set before him endured the cross, scorning its shame, and sat down at the right hand of the throne of God.' (Hebrews 12:1-2)

It is vital that we find the right target to aim for so we can achieve the prize we want to win.

My sense of purpose is what has helped me get through the difficult periods of my Christian walk when all else seemed hopeless. The assurance that God had a plan for my life and a strategy for me to follow empowered me to overcome even the highest hurdles and gave me a reason to fight against all odds. Purpose also motivates me to achieve my ultimate calling and become everything God means me to be; it strengthens my core beliefs and moral foundation, particularly as the world around me goes through radical changes, and it has fired up the very depths of my soul to be a warrior for the kingdom of God.

When God placed His hand on my life it was obvious that I had to deal with 'stuff', or 'baggage'. As we know, baggage is heavy to lug around; it weighs us down and is a real burden.

A few years ago Lesley and I bought our home (well, the bank did!). It was much smaller than the previous home we had been renting. We had so much stuff that we had to leave much of it still boxed in the garage. After a number of years it is still there and we have not missed it or wanted to use any of it. The baggage in life can be like all these boxes sitting in the garage. We carry it around with us, refusing to discard it as we feel we can't live without it. It can become like an anchor, which stops us moving forward into everything that God has purposed for our lives.

My prayer for you is that you'll discard the baggage that's anchoring you down so you can move forward and attain the goals God has set before you. I pray you will find the purpose and meaning of your life in Jesus.

The distinguished Scottish writer Thomas Carlyle reflected back on his life saying, 'The older I grow – and I now stand on the brink of eternity – the more comes back to me that sentence in the Catechism which I learned when a child, and the fuller and deeper its meaning becomes: "What is the chief end of man? To glorify God and enjoy Him forever."'

Healing for anything, whether spirit, soul or body, is God's business. Just be faithful in the little things God asks of you and He will look after the big things.

In Closing

A friend of mine who had been to a meeting came and told me some of the things they had discussed. A salesman from a very well known Australian company had addressed the gathering, and one statement had stuck in my friend's mind. 'You never give anything away cheap,' the salesman said, 'because it reflects on your product.'

The first thing that crossed my mind was that God our Father gave His Son for us. The price was not cheap but priceless, because it reflected the product, which is you and me. This is how valuable we are to God.

If there is anything I want this book to do, it is to encourage you into seeking God – and if you are a father, please take up and fulfil the role as best you can. God has taken my life, which was a total mess, and turned it into an incredible message of hope for those who struggle with homosexuality and for those living with HIV. He is also calling men to be men. I am not the only man God has done this for, and you may be asking yourself why you are reading this right now. Perhaps God is tapping the window of your heart to see whether you will respond to Him, as He is the God of all hope.

I often look back over the years to see how far He has brought me, and I stand in awe of His grace and mercy and His incredible life changing power. The wonderful thing about it all is that it is not just for a chosen few but for everyone. There have been times when my walk has had its difficulties, when I have responded to Him out of frustration, but when I look at the Scriptures I see that where this is concerned I'm only one in a long queue.

At the start of Psalm 77 Asaph is going through a hard time and is complaining bitterly. Then in verse 10 he takes hold of himself, remembers what the Lord has done for him in the past and turns his despair to praise:

'Then I thought, "To this I will appeal: the years of the right hand of the Most High." I will remember the deeds of the LORD; yes, I will remember your miracles of long ago. I will meditate on all your works and consider all your mighty deeds. Your ways, O God, are holy. What god is so great as our God? You are the God who performs miracles; you display your power among the peoples. (Psalm 77:10-14)

The walk and progressive restoration continues from recovery to discovery (I love that saying!) and looks forward to taking hold of all God's promises.

The apostle Paul writes in Philippians 3:12-14, 'Not that I have already obtained all this, or have already been made perfect, but I press on to take hold of that for which Christ Jesus took hold of me. Brothers, I do not consider myself yet to have taken hold of it. But one thing I do: Forgetting what is behind and straining toward what is ahead I press on towards the goal to win the prize for which God has called me heavenwards in Christ Jesus.'

All along the course of my journey I have had to face tests. Some I have passed and some I have not, but throughout it all those trials have been turned into testimonies of how great our Saviour Jesus is. What began as failures God has turned into victories that resound with His power and His love for His people, and I can only stand amazed at the sovereign way He took hold of my life and transformed me from a homosexual into a husband.

QUOTATIONS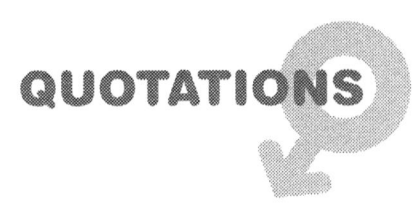

Taken from N.S.W. Assembly of God State Conference
By Paul de Jong
Copyright © 2003
Used by permission of Paul de Jong.

Taken from "Same Sex Partnerships?"
By John Stott
Copyright © 1998
Used by permission of Zondervan.

Taken from "Homosexuality: A New Christian Ethic"
By Elizabeth R. Moberley
Copyright © 1983
Used by permission of James Clark & Co.

Taken from the introductory text to the
Album "Palabras de Fuego" - Words of Fire
Released 1999
By Diego Souto
Copyright © 1999
Used by permission of Diego Souto.

www.ingramcontent.com/pod-product-compliance
Lightning Source LLC
Chambersburg PA
CBHW020910090426
42736CB00008B/563